Get the Net!

THE CRAZED FLY FISHERMAN'S CATALOG

Virtual Reality Trout Stream
$56,000

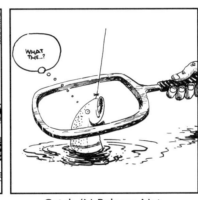

Catch 'N Release Net
$90

Exploding Fly
$20

Jack Ohman

WILLOW CREEK PRESS

Minocqua, Wisconsin

Published by   WILLOW CREEK PRESS
P.O. Box 147
Minocqua, WI 54548

For information on other Willow Creek Press titles,
call 1-800-850-WILD

Library of Congress Cataloging-in-Publication Data
Ohman, Jack.
      Get the Net! : the crazed fly fisherman's catalog / Jack Ohman.
         p.   cm.
      ISBN 1-57223-120-3 (alk. paper)
      1. Fly fishing--Humor. 2. Fly fishing--Caricatures and cartoons.
3. American wit and humor, Pictorial. I. Title.
PN6231.F620365   1997
799.1'24'0207--dc21   97-22426
                                                                    CIP

Printed in the United States of America

Trademarks and the products they accompany are fictitious.
Products not sold in stores, or on TV, or (we hope) anywhere.

INTRODUCTION

Nine years ago, I wrote a book called *Fear of Fly Fishing*. *Fear of Fly Fishing* is the only book I have ever written that has made a profit or was a best seller.

When I first wrote *Fear of Fly fishing*, I realized that I actually knew very little about fly fishing. This was a major concern to me, because a deadline loomed. But an even greater concern was that I realized that I wasn't fishing enough. This horrifying realization became an obsession that I began to rectify with almost weekly trips with a guy named Jim Ramsey, who is truly a psychotic fly fisherman. I supplemented those trips with others, such as Dick Thomas, who is a merely manic fly fisherman. And then I started to pay to fly fish with people like Rich McIntyre, who defies psychological clinical definition.

Pretty soon, I realized that not only was I fishing enough, I was fishing too much. I began to subscribe to four different fly fishing magazines. I built a rod. I tied my own leaders. I learned to tie flies. I began talking to my wife — long-suffering does not scratch the surface here — about fly fishing and its larger implications on our vacations plans, as in "We can't go there. It takes an hour to get to any decent water," or "That place is no good. Too many masking hatches."

After a few years, I began to "accidentally" buy equipment I already had. Heck, who doesn't need eight Sage rods in weights ranging from 2 to 6, and a couple of cane rods? And a pack rod. And three (for God's sake) fly tying vises? You get the drag-free drift. Then I started conjuring humorous fly fishing gadgets. What scares me is that some of these may actually exist. What really scares me is that you may have bought some of them. So open up your wallet, and leave your VISA number at the door.

Jack Ohman, Portland, Oregon

WISEGUY FROM JERSEY GUIDE KILLER®

Who hasn't wanted to kill their guide? Guides are rude weisenheimers just waiting for an opportunity to make you look stupid. They make cutting remarks about your casting ability, criticize your ensembles, and piss and moan constantly about their tip. Who needs it? Take out your guide with a Wiseguy From Jersey Guide Killer®. A real Wiseguy from Jersey will make sure that mean-spirited guide sleeps with the fishes — big time. Don't ask any more questions.

Price: To be arranged.

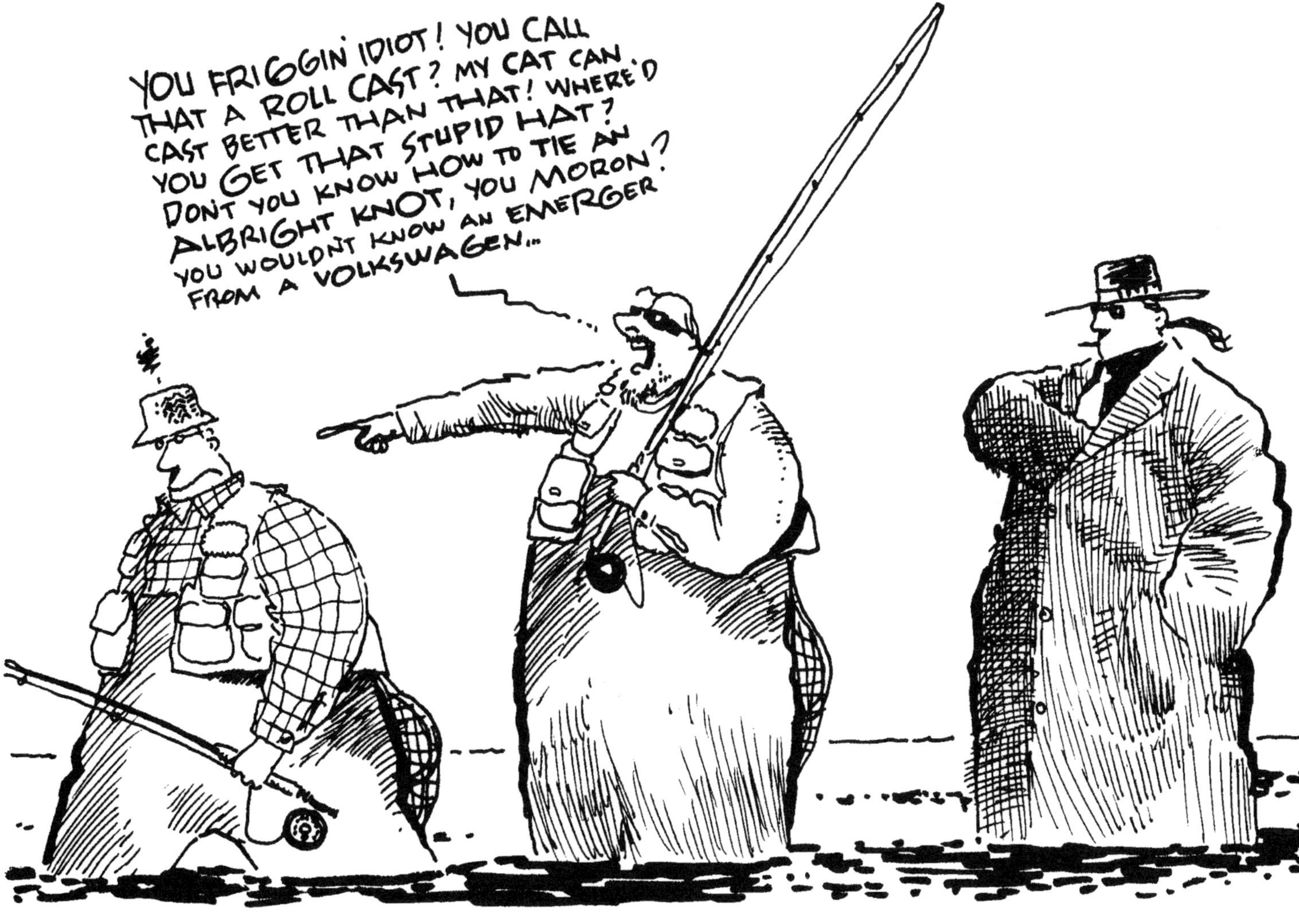
YOU FRIGGIN' IDIOT! YOU CALL THAT A ROLL CAST? MY CAT CAN CAST BETTER THAN THAT! WHERE'D YOU GET THAT STUPID HAT? DONT YOU KNOW HOW TO TIE AN ALBRIGHT KNOT, YOU MORON? YOU WOULDN'T KNOW AN EMERGER FROM A VOLKSWAGEN...

THE LET'S CALL A SPADE A SPADE STRIKE INDICATOR®

The debate rages on: are strike indicators sporting? Or are they just, well, bobbers for people who involve themselves in complicated delusions? The Let's Call a Spade a Spade Strike Indicator® leaves no doubt in anyone's mind just where you stand on the issue. The Let's Call a Spade a Spade Strike Indicator® is big, red and white, and floats like those massive plastic orbs you see on the lines of all those bank fishermen. It really, really works, and makes a statement about just where you stand on this life and death question of our times.

Color: White top, red bottom.
Price: 39 cents.
Available at all lower-middle-class sporting goods outlets and hardware stores.

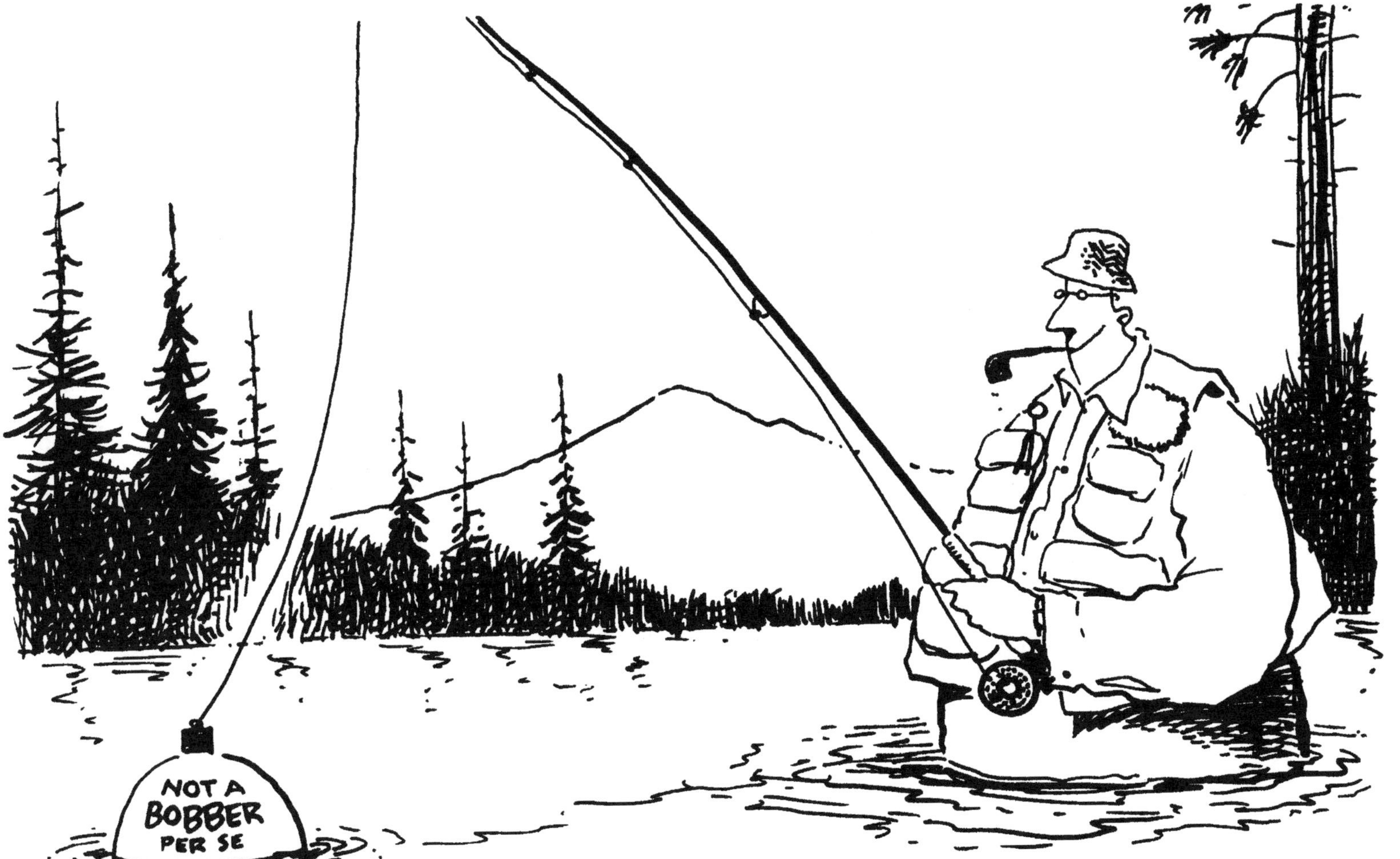
NOT A
BOBBER
PER SE

THE EXPLODING FLY®

You've rifled your fly box dozens of times, trying to get that perfect fly to match the hatch, but nothing seems to work. Even when you seemingly have the "right" fly, you can't connect. It's time for the equalizer: The Exploding Fly®. With the Exploding Fly®, you're on the way to a hooking percentage of one hundred percent. The Exploding Fly® concept is simple: a tiny but deadly dab of C-4 plastique dubbing material turns an ordinary fly into a trout search and destroy mission. Catch even short-striking trout and sippers. In fact, any trout within a ten-foot radius of the Exploding Fly® is yours; a flick of the wrist detonates the charge. Makes catch and release a difficult proposition, however.

Available in all known patterns, except the Parmachene Belle. Extreme caution should be used when handling flies larger than size eight. Finger loss may result. Do not cast near open flame or in temperatures above 85 degrees.
Price: $20 per fly.

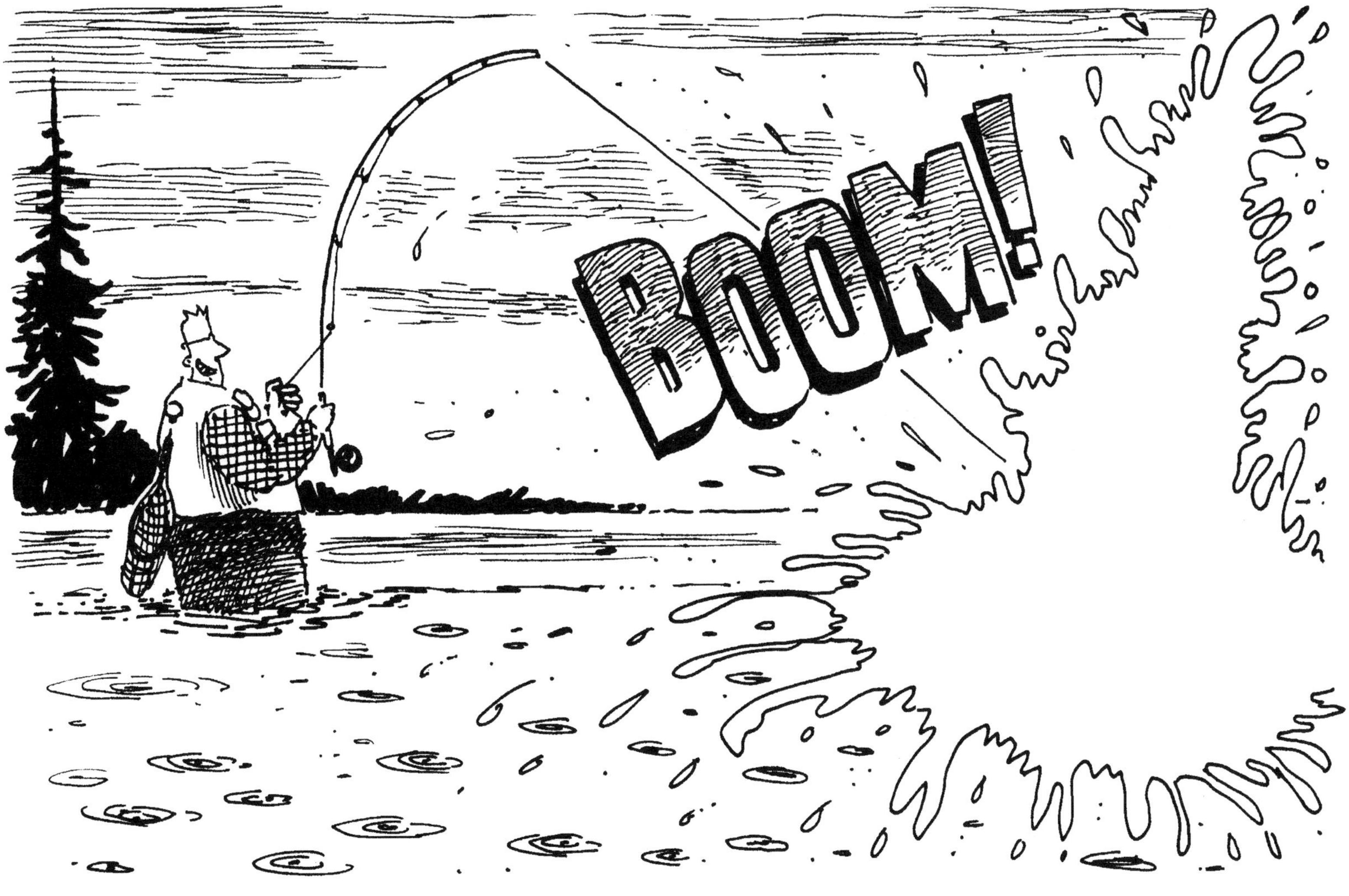
BOOM!

RESCUE 911 TROUT TRAMA TRIAGE UNIT®

Oh, sure, catch and release is the way to go; everyone agrees on that. But don't you wish you could help revive the trout with a little more than wiggling its tail in the water? Swing into action with the Rescue 911 Trout Trama Triage Unit®. You've got everything you need to save your trout on the spot. Magnetic Resonance Imaging at streamside isolates the injury. You diagnose the trauma: barbed hook injury? Foul hooking? Maybe even a little blood? You save the trout with your sterilized forceps and laser scalpel. Respirator keeps the trout alive while you work feverishly over the soon-to-be-released patient. Medicaid, Medicare, Single Payer National Health Care Plans not included.

Cost: Uncontained.

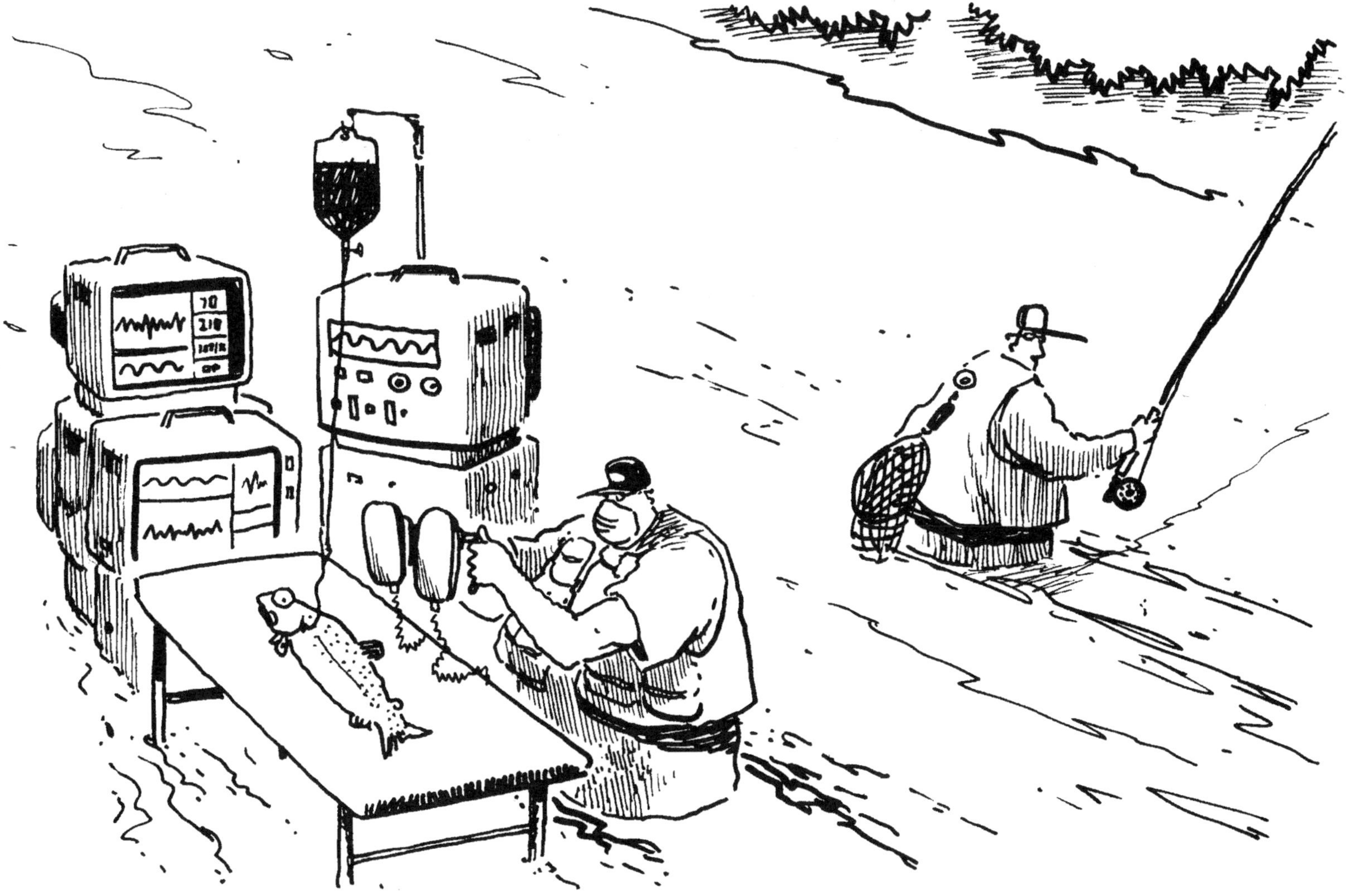

THE ARROGANT ANGLER® MAGAZINE

The *Arrogant Angler*® magazine. Subscribe to the snottiest fly fishing magazine around. Saul Bellow on strike indicators. Bill Moyers on neoprene. Tom Wolfe on reel seats. Norman Mailer on belly boats. Extensive background check (financial disclosure, family lineage) will let you know within two years if you've been selected for a lottery to be eligible to subscribe. They'll call you.

Price: $19.99 per issue, if you're lucky.

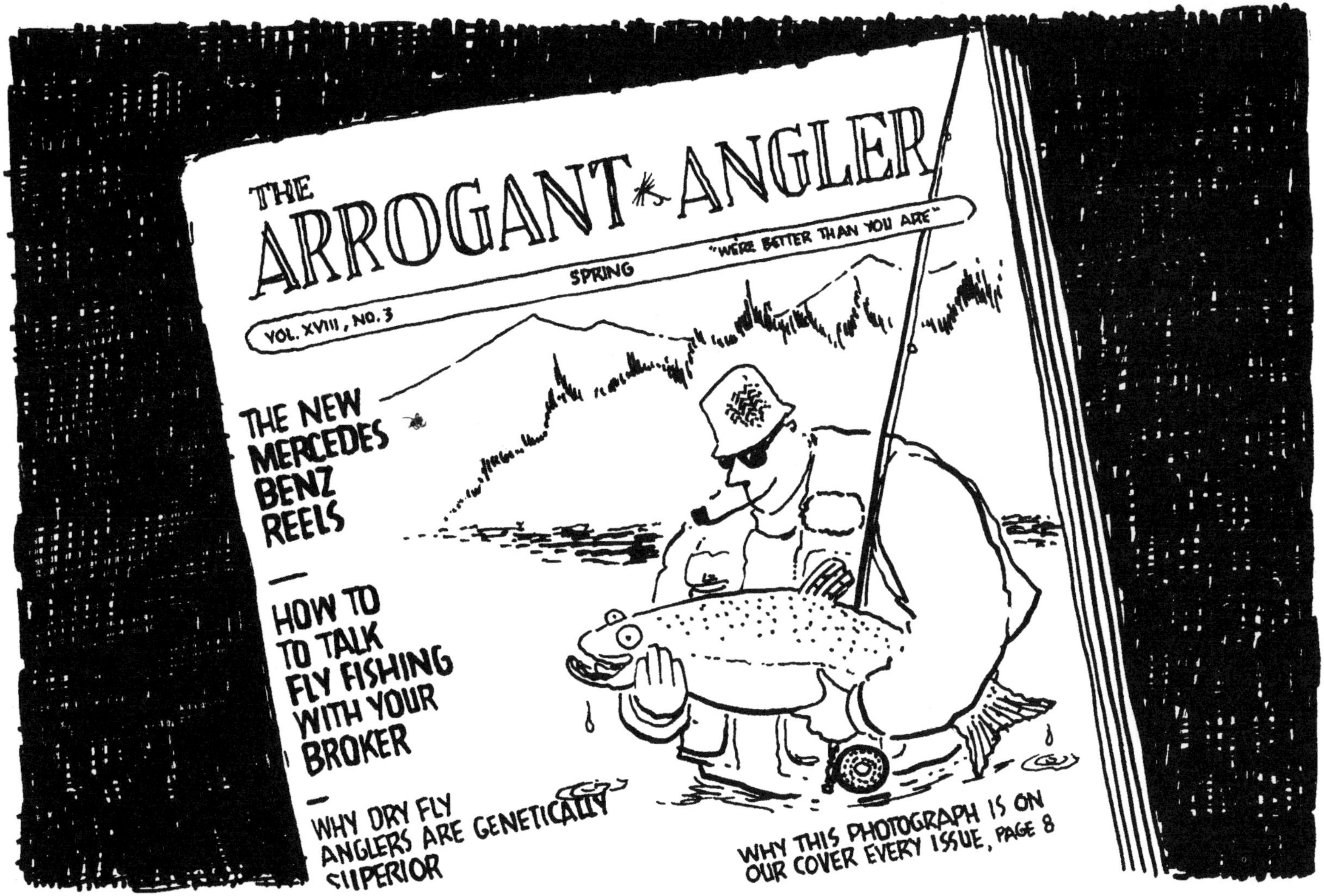
THE ARROGANT ANGLER
"WE'RE BETTER THAN YOU ARE"
SPRING
VOL. XVIII, NO. 3
THE NEW MERCEDES BENZ REELS
HOW TO TO TALK FLY FISHING WITH YOUR BROKER
WHY DRY FLY ANGLERS ARE GENETICALLY SUPERIOR
WHY THIS PHOTOGRAPH IS ON OUR COVER EVERY ISSUE, PAGE 8

CHINESE RE-EDUCATION FISHING CAMP

This deluxe trip package will break you of all your bad fly fishing habits and you'll come away with a new understanding of Marxist doctrine through the help of experienced Chinese "guides." You'll fish the Yalu, which doesn't contain any trout, but who cares? You'll spend your days memorizing the Thoughts of Chairman Mao while performing back-breaking soul and brain-cleansing revolutionary work, like tying leaders and building cane rods from bamboo on the very riverbank you'll be fishing. You'll come away from the trip thinner, fishless, and ready to spread the gospel of Chinese revolutionary thought.

Price: Six months, $90. Includes rice and a somewhat boxy uniform.

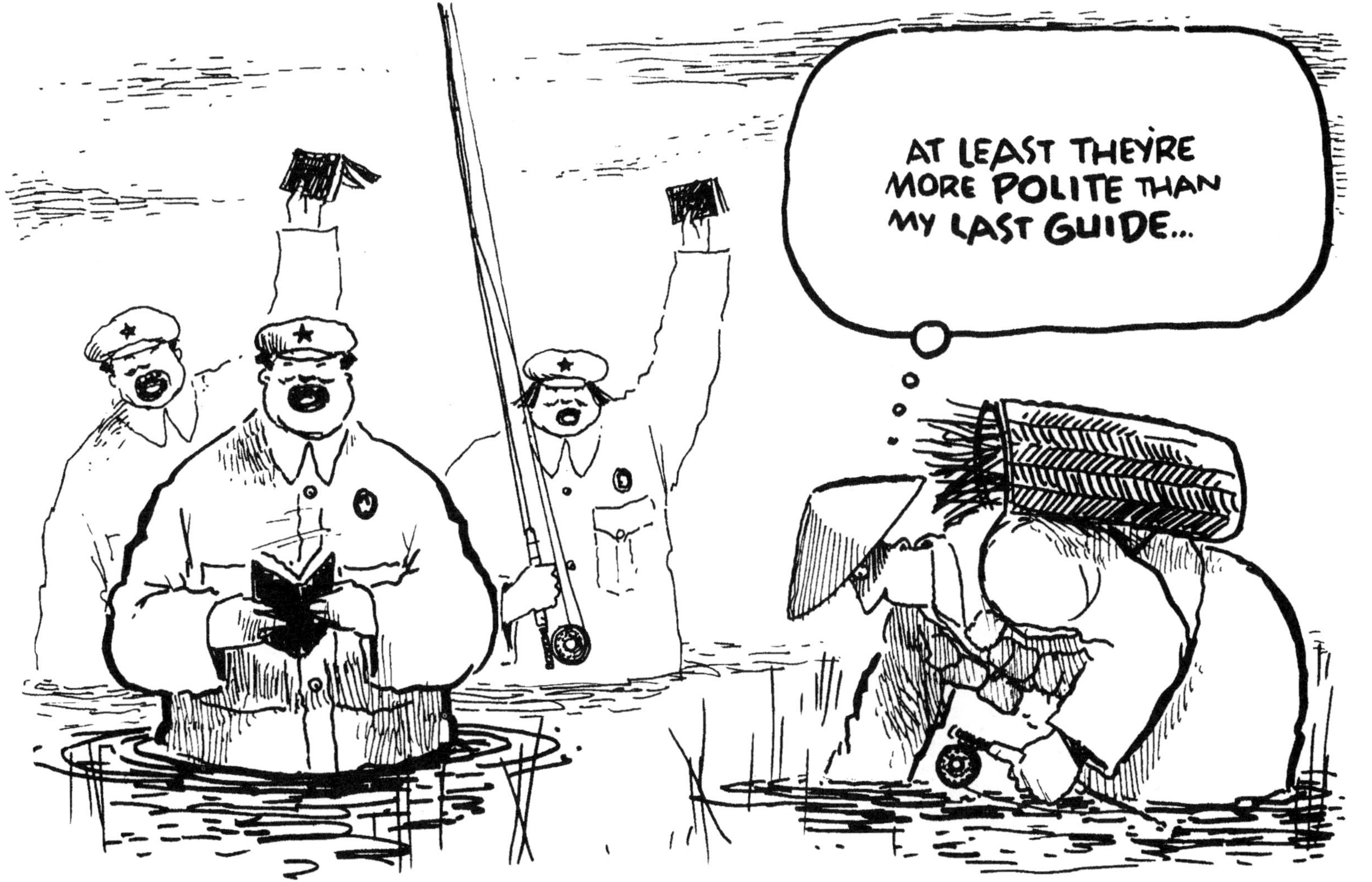
AT LEAST THEY'RE MORE POLITE THAN MY LAST GUIDE...

TOXIC WASTE SUPERFUND SITE FISHING EXPEDITIONS

Urban anglers rejoice! Now you can fish those convenient Superfund toxic waste sites. Thanks to a generous grant from the Environmental Protection Agency, those squalid, putrescent slime holes have become top-notch trout habitat. You'll have miles of "water" all to yourself as you stalk slightly irradiated trout. Love Canal is now one of America's premier angling destinations! It's accessible and generally will not melt your leader. Remember, don't smoke near the stream and whatever you do, don't touch the trout. Unless you want your life expectancy to drop twenty-nine years.

Price: $50 per rod per decade.

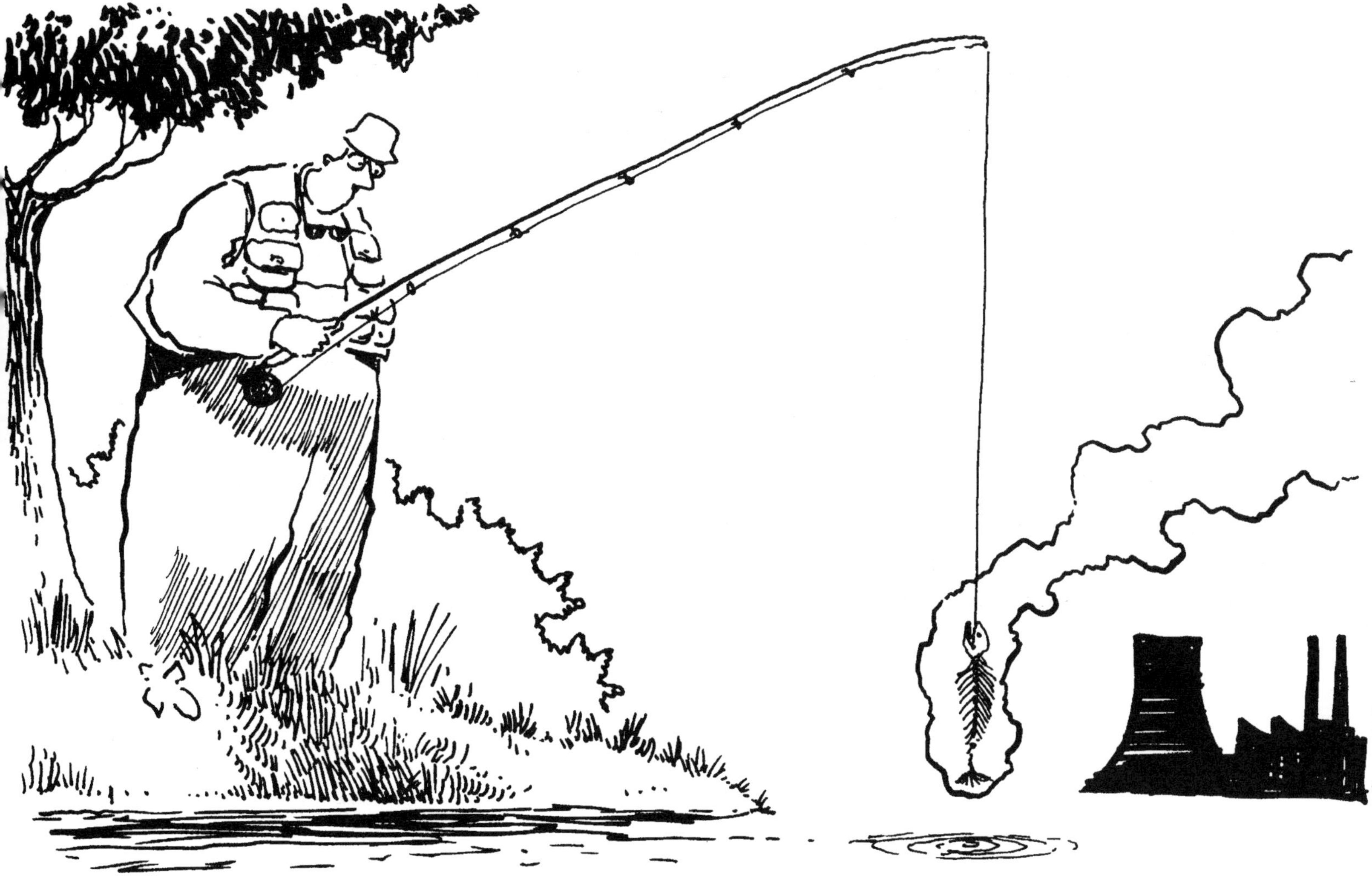

THE ULTIMATE FLY FISHING DESTINATION: MARS!!

First, there was New Zealand. Then, the former Soviet Union. Now, Mars! With the discovery that life once existed on Mars, the National Aeronautics and Space Administration, in conjunction with Zero G Tours, has put together the trip of a fishing lifetime: the Red Planet. You'll fish the canals of Mars using the very latest graphite rods and pressurized Simms waders. You'll thrill to the knowledge that you're fishing for organisms that have been dead for over three billion years. Hey, what river hasn't seemed that way on earth? Transportation's no problem, either; not with the still-mighty Saturn V launch vehicle and the space station Freedom (due to be completed early April 2018). Plan on a fifteen-month one-way trip, two-week American/Martian Plan accommodations, and don't bring any unnecessary weight.

Price: $900 billion.

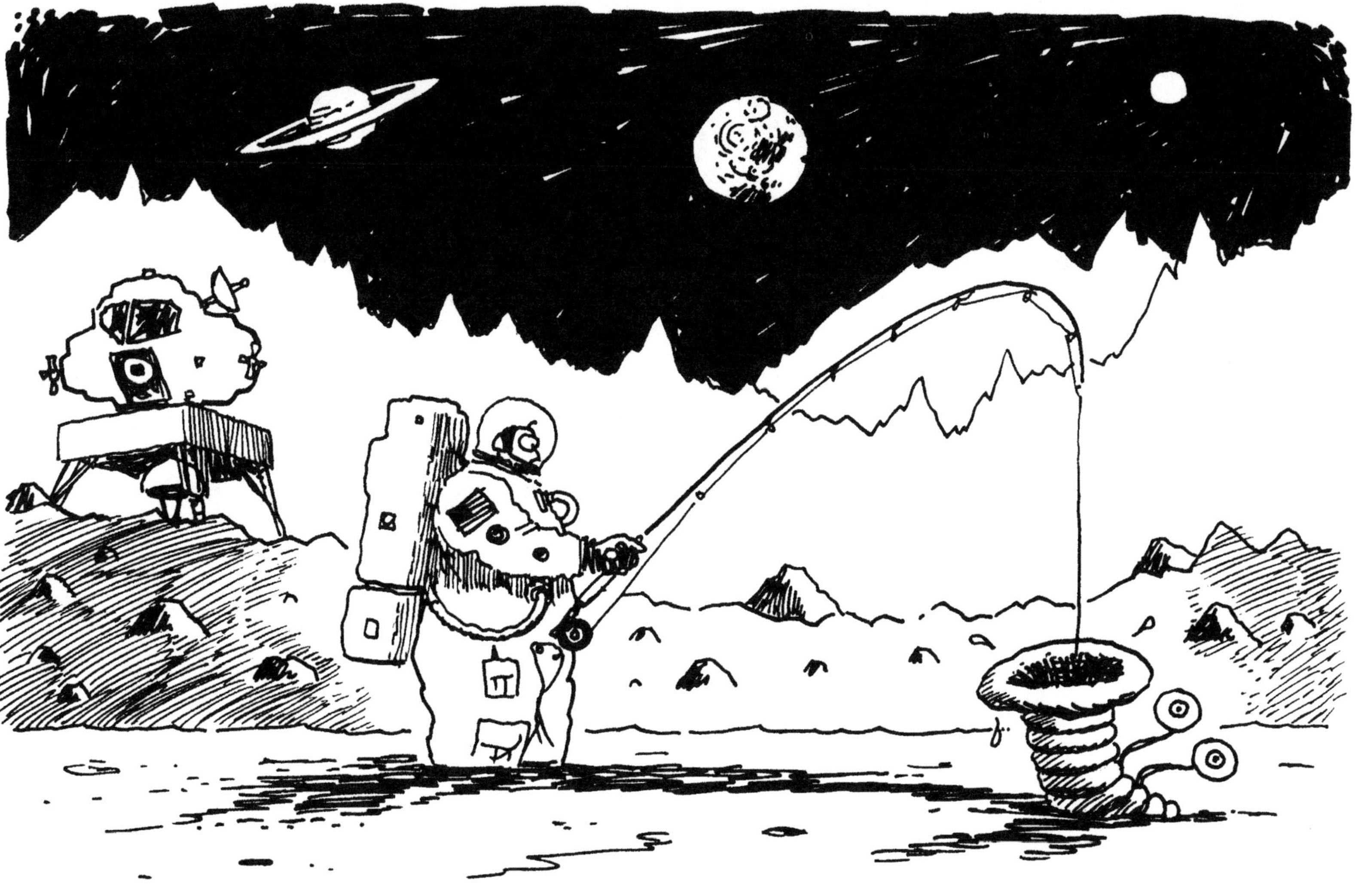

TEACH YOUR DOG TO FLY FISH
INSTRUCTIONAL VIDEO®

Why let hunters have all the fun with dogs? You can teach your dog to fly fish with six one-hour instructional videos! This series will show your dog the mechanics of fly casting and the science of matching the hatch. Not only that, the videos will teach Fido the True Secret of Fly Fishing Mastery: opposable thumbs. You'll marvel at Spot's progress as he not only hooks a trout, but fetches him as well. Narrated by Lassie.

May not be suitable for some easily agitated breeds, like pit bulls or poodles. Rolled up newpaper included.
Price: $129.95.

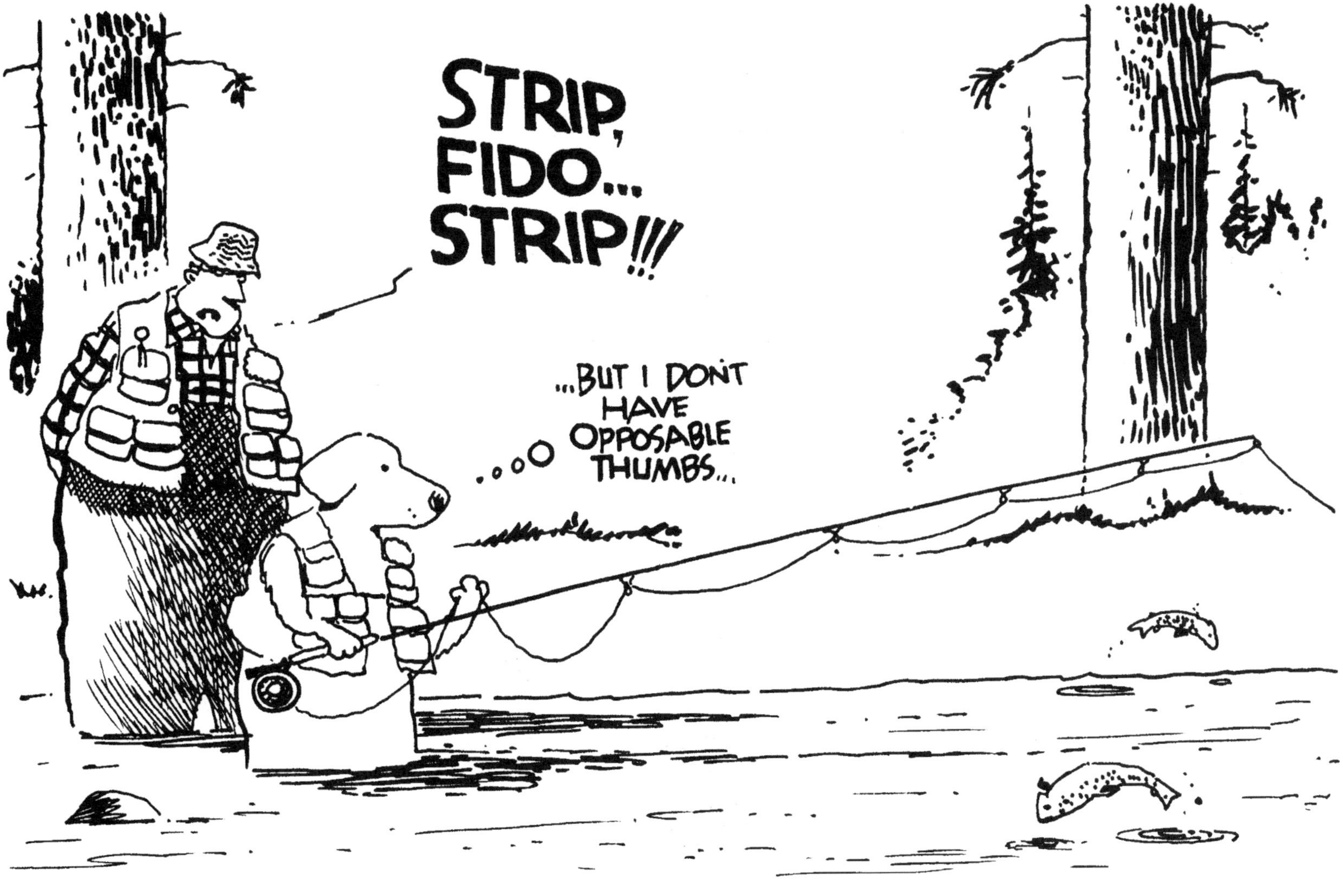
STRIP, FIDO... STRIP!!!
...BUT I DON'T HAVE OPPOSABLE THUMBS...

BACKCAST AREA CLEARING UNIT®

What's more annoying than a pod of fish rising situated directly in front of an impenetrable tangle of underbrush and trees with no place to backcast? Solve the problem. With extreme prejudice. The Backcast Area Clearing Unit® operates on six AA batteries and two gallons of pure napalm. Treelines and brambles evaporate in seconds, and you've got a clear if unsightly casting alley that has you fishing in seconds. Straps on any vest and you're in business. Use with caution.

Avoid being startled by your fishing partners, for example.
Price: $9900.

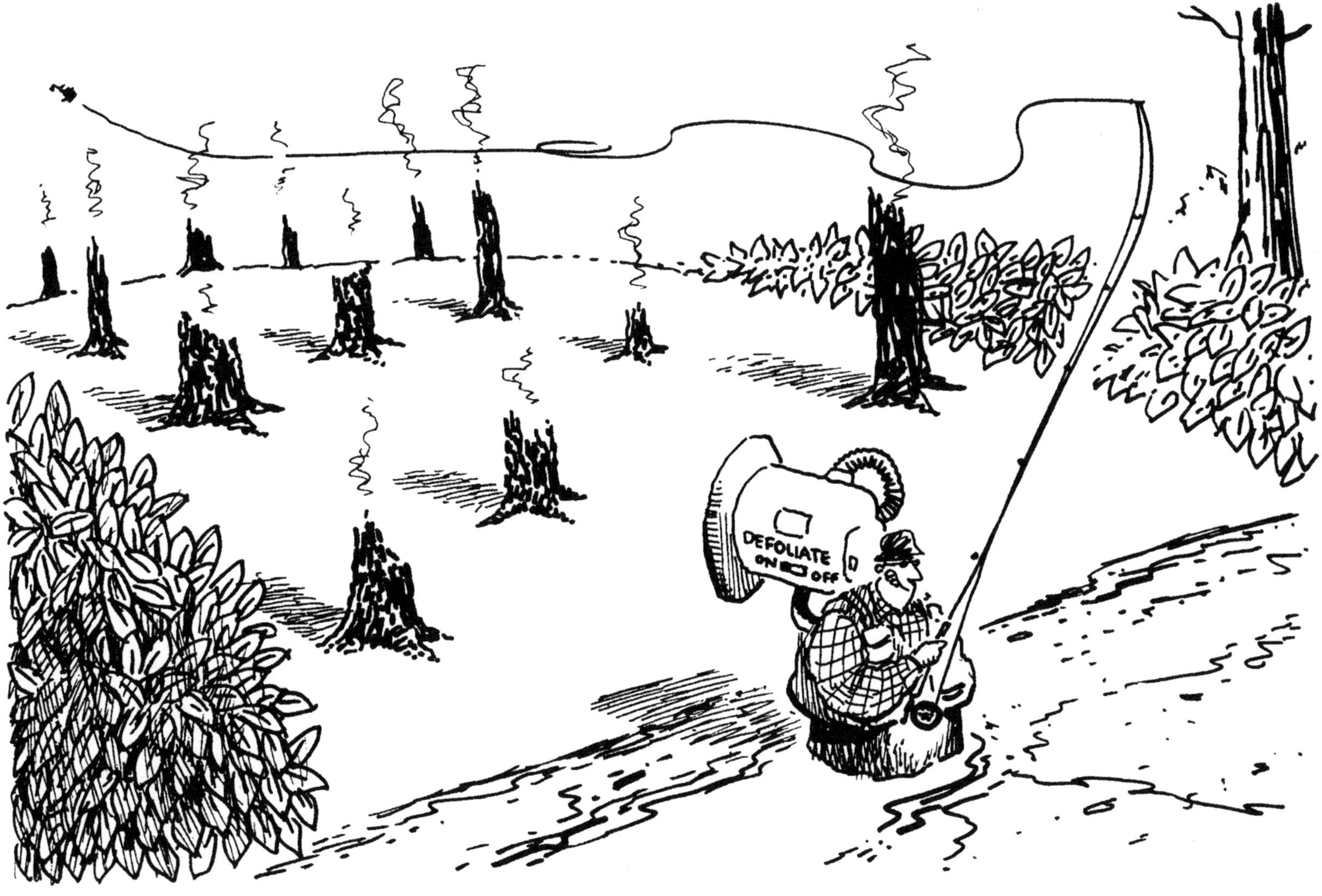
DEFOLIATE
ON OFF

LARGE TROUT EMERGENCY AIRBAG®

When you've hooked the big one, and it actually poses a danger to your physical well-being, you want the Large Trout Emergency Airbag® from the Chrysler Corporation. Ever taken a tail in the chops? Neither have we, but it could happen. The Large Trout Emergency Airbag® automatically inflates when a trout 22 inches or longer gets within two feet of the angler. When it deploys, watch out! The bag's going over 200 mph, so you better not be into catch and release. Not for anglers under 6'6" and 230 pounds. Do not attempt to disconnect.

Price: $1599.

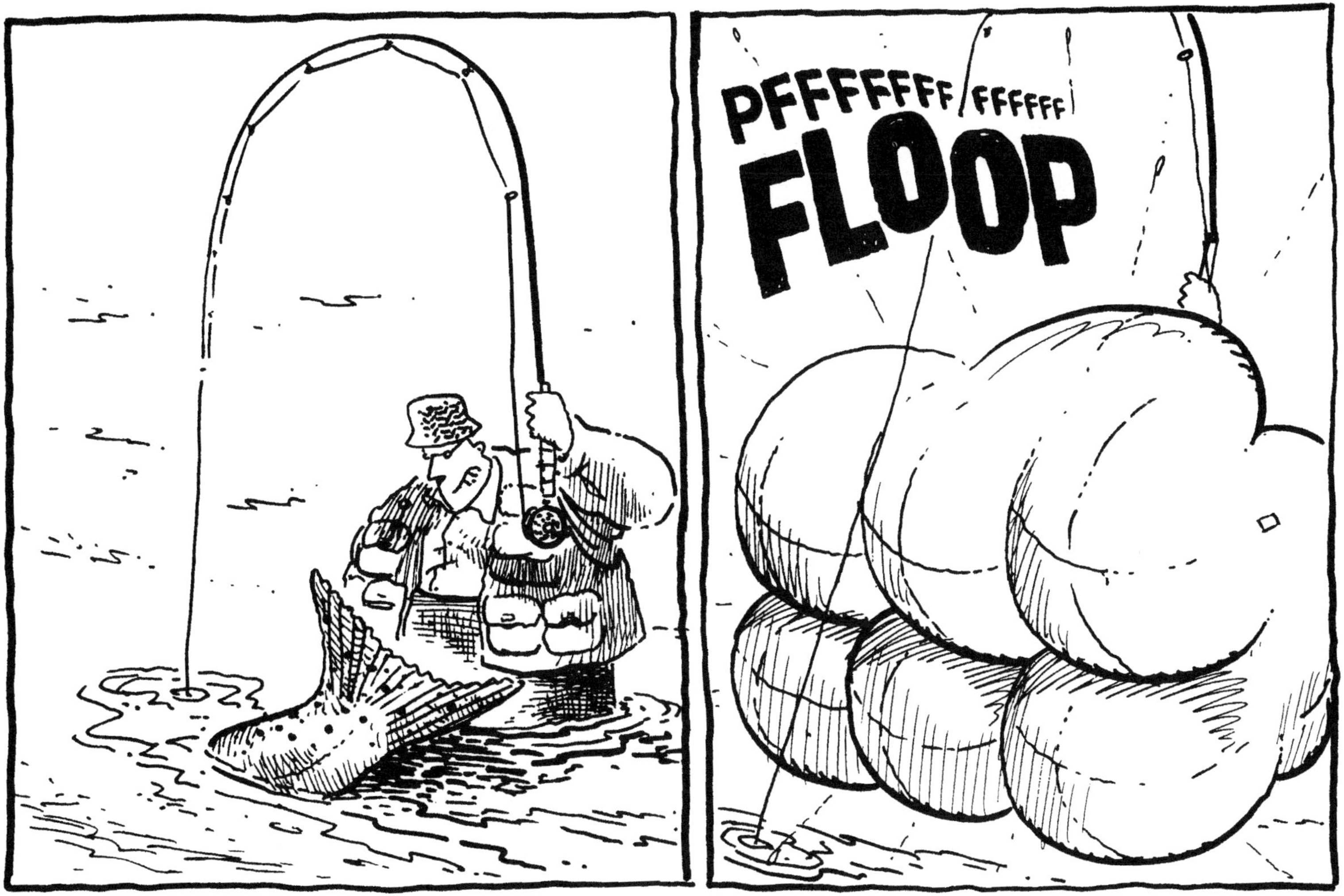
PFFFFFFF FFFFFF
FLOOP

FLY FISHING IN THE ROUGH®

Did you know you can use modern fly fishing techniques to catch and release (please don't, in this case) jumbo trash fish on our nation's great rivers that don't hold trout? Did you know that a carp will rise to an Adams if you dip it in pure pork lard? Or that a nymph shaped like a doughball will take sucker after sucker, even in tough stream conditions, such as the river being on fire? It's true, and more. Learn how a Chevy bumper painted like a Cream Cahill drives eelpout nuts. Thrill to the rise of a thirty-eight pound carp as it mistakes a fly for a Hostess Twinkie. This kit includes all you'll need to start catching rough fish on fly gear: lard, grease, dough, entrails, and all sorts of glop you wouldn't feed to a pig will have you wading in big trash fish before you know it.

Price: absolutely free.

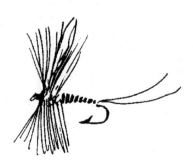

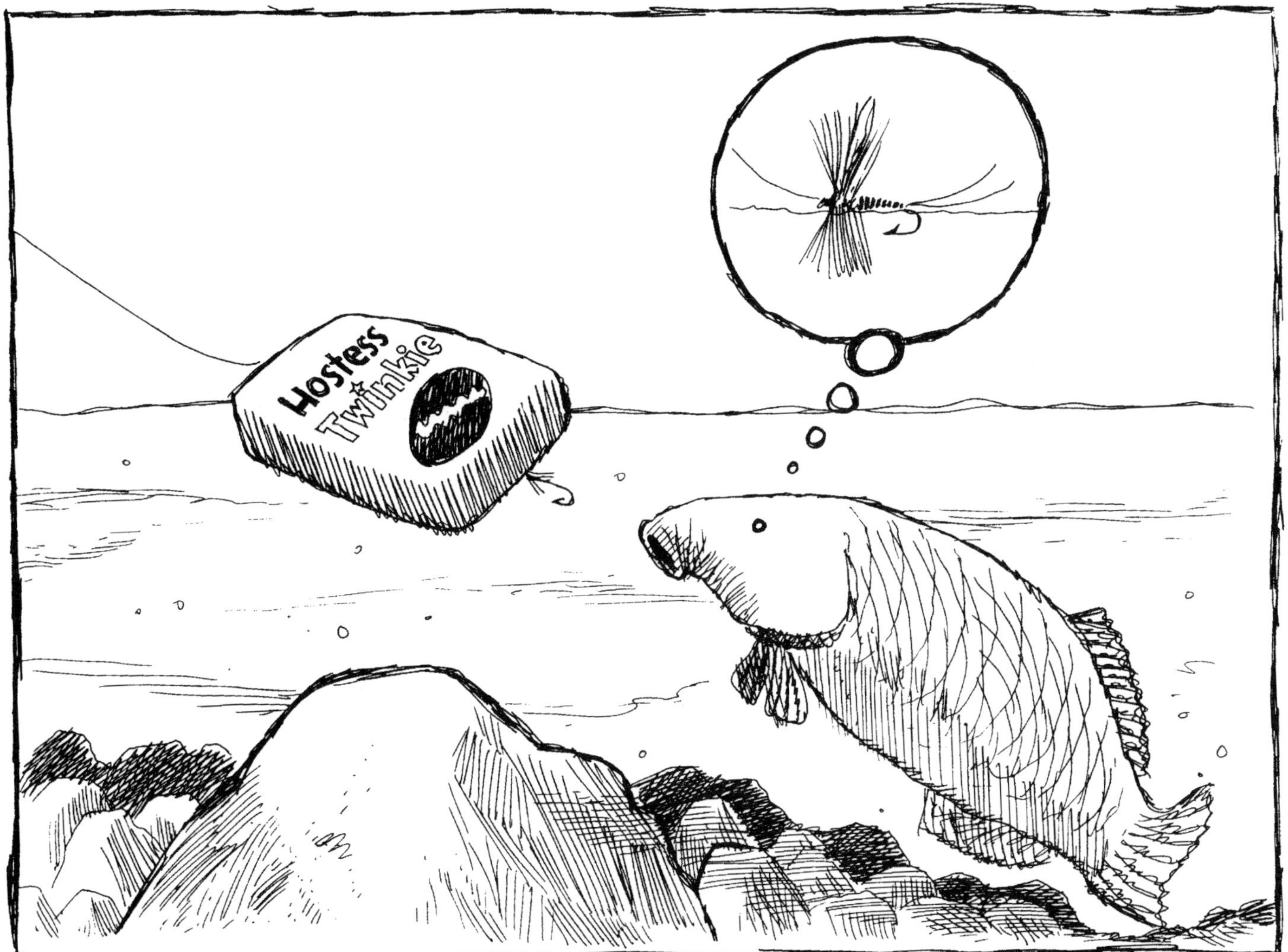
Hostess
Twinkie

FLY FISHING FRIENDS®

You've probably noticed that the split-second you start talking about fly fishing, non-flyfishermen roll their eyes back into their head and quickly look for the nearest emergency exits. That's why you need a Fly Fishing Friend®. A Fly Fishing Friend® will gab all day about tippet material and fly line sink rates. Fly Fishing Friends® will jabber incessantly about caddis pupa emergers, river levels, complicated knots, and leader diameters. A Fly Fishing Friend® will talk endlessly about neoprene thickness, graphite rod loading capacities, and the porosity of dubbing material. A Fly Fishing Friend® is like any friend, except he won't bore you with the details and complications of his real life troubles, like the state of his relationship with a woman, his tax bracket, or why his boss is a bastard. Fly Fishing Friends® are available in both sexes and all races and even fishing ability, ranging from egg pattern chucker to size 26 cream midge cane rod fascist.

Price: $4.00/hour.

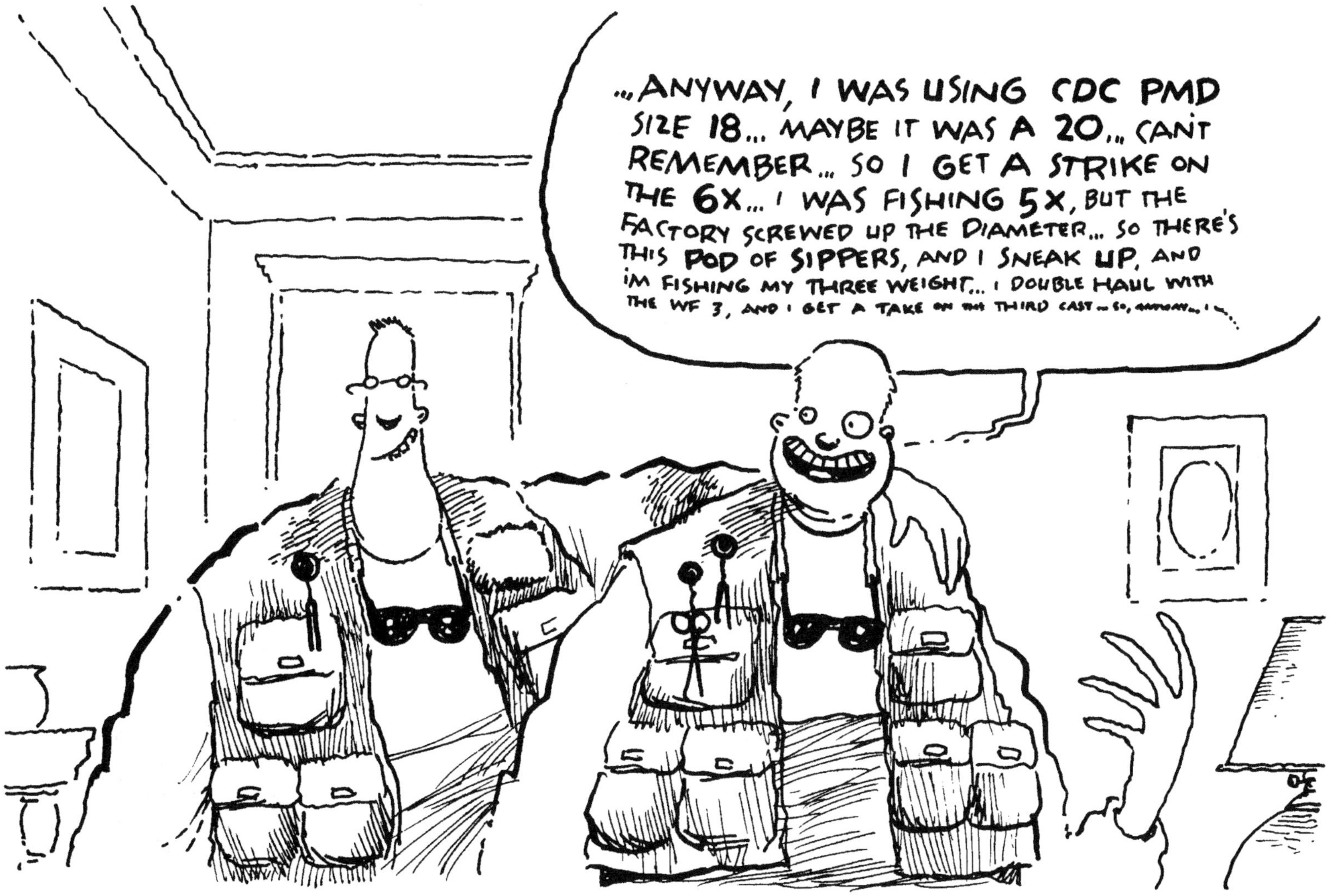
...ANYWAY, I WAS USING CDC PMD SIZE 18... MAYBE IT WAS A 20... CAN'T REMEMBER... SO I GET A STRIKE ON THE 6X... I WAS FISHING 5X, BUT THE FACTORY SCREWED UP THE DIAMETER... SO THERE'S THIS POD OF SIPPERS, AND I SNEAK UP, AND I'M FISHING MY THREE WEIGHT... I DOUBLE HAUL WITH THE WF 3, AND I GET A TAKE ON THE THIRD CAST... SO, ANYWAY... I...

BUSINESS TROUTWEAR®

It's hard to break away from the office, physically as well as psychologically. Therapists tell us that it's unwise to go from one extreme experience to the next without a transitional period. That's where Business Troutwear®, from Hookey-Freeman Streamside Tailors comes in. If you can't make the break entirely from work, or simply don't have time to change clothes on the way from your high-pressure business job to the river, just button-up and button down in the conservative yet functional trout fishing clothing that will make you look both crisply traditional yet ready to roll and roll cast. First, step into the blue pinstripe or gray flannel two button single vent neoprene two piece suit. A white button down neoprene shirt and rep striped fleece tie (perfect for hanging dozens of drying flies) is your fashionable yet muted look, ready for the boardroom or the spinner fall. Special felt soled wingtip wading shoes complete the ensemble. Wear it to work and never worry about spilling that coffee again. Sizes 38-48. Not available in camouflage.

Suit: $895. Shoes: $250. Tie: $85.

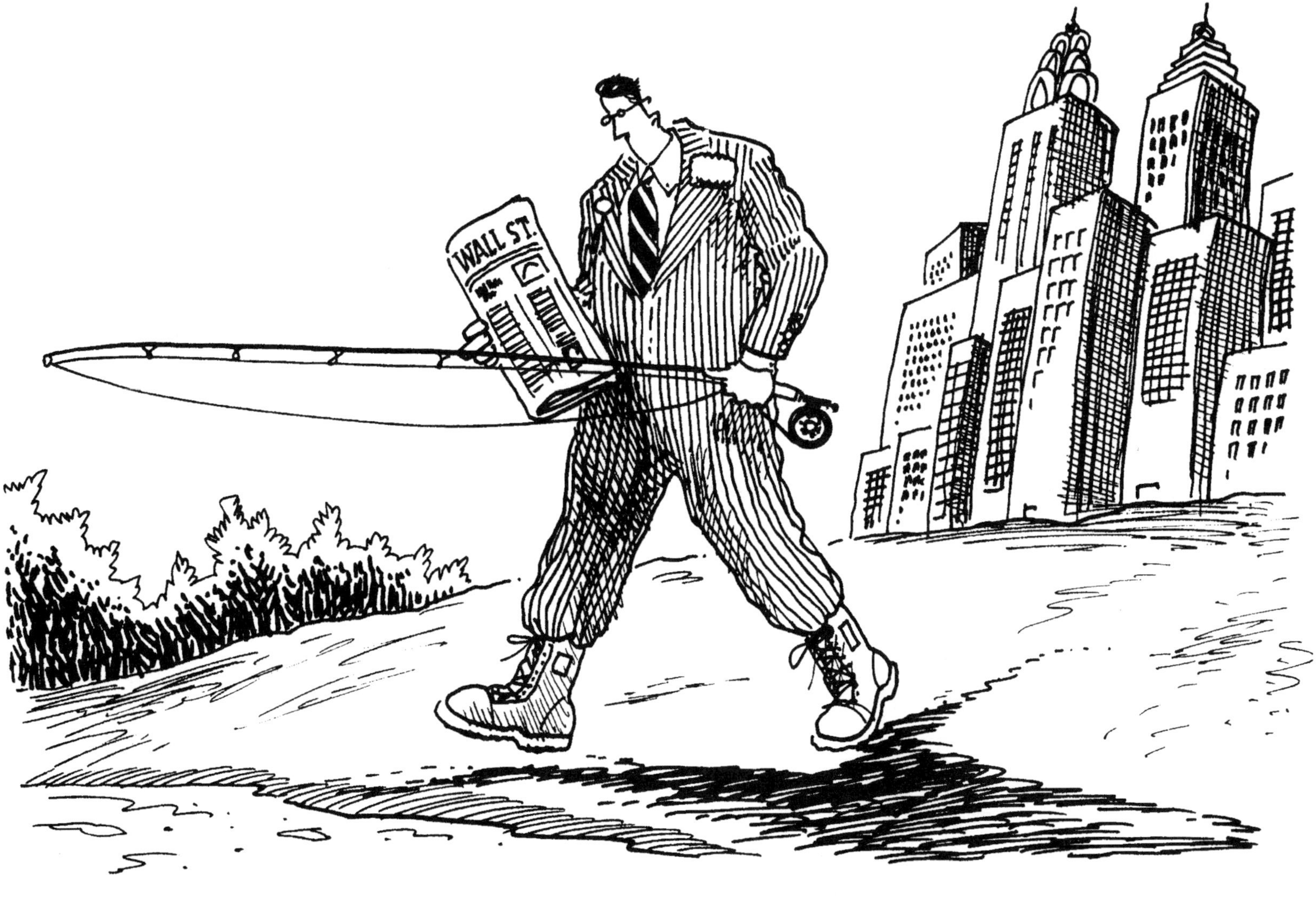
WALL ST.

THE MULTIPLE ROD®

How many times have you seen fifty fish rising simultaneously, and just couldn't cover them fast enough? The Multiple Rod® is the definitive answer. Using three shafts of graphite on one easy reverse wells handle, the Multiple Rod® takes some getting used to, but, hey, it's not like you don't get your line tangled up already. Roll cast, double haul and dapple while you hook fish after fish. Requires two AA batteries and the manual dexterity of Dr. Michael DeBakey. Some assembly required. Multiple line weights may cause injury or death.

Price: $1,699.99.

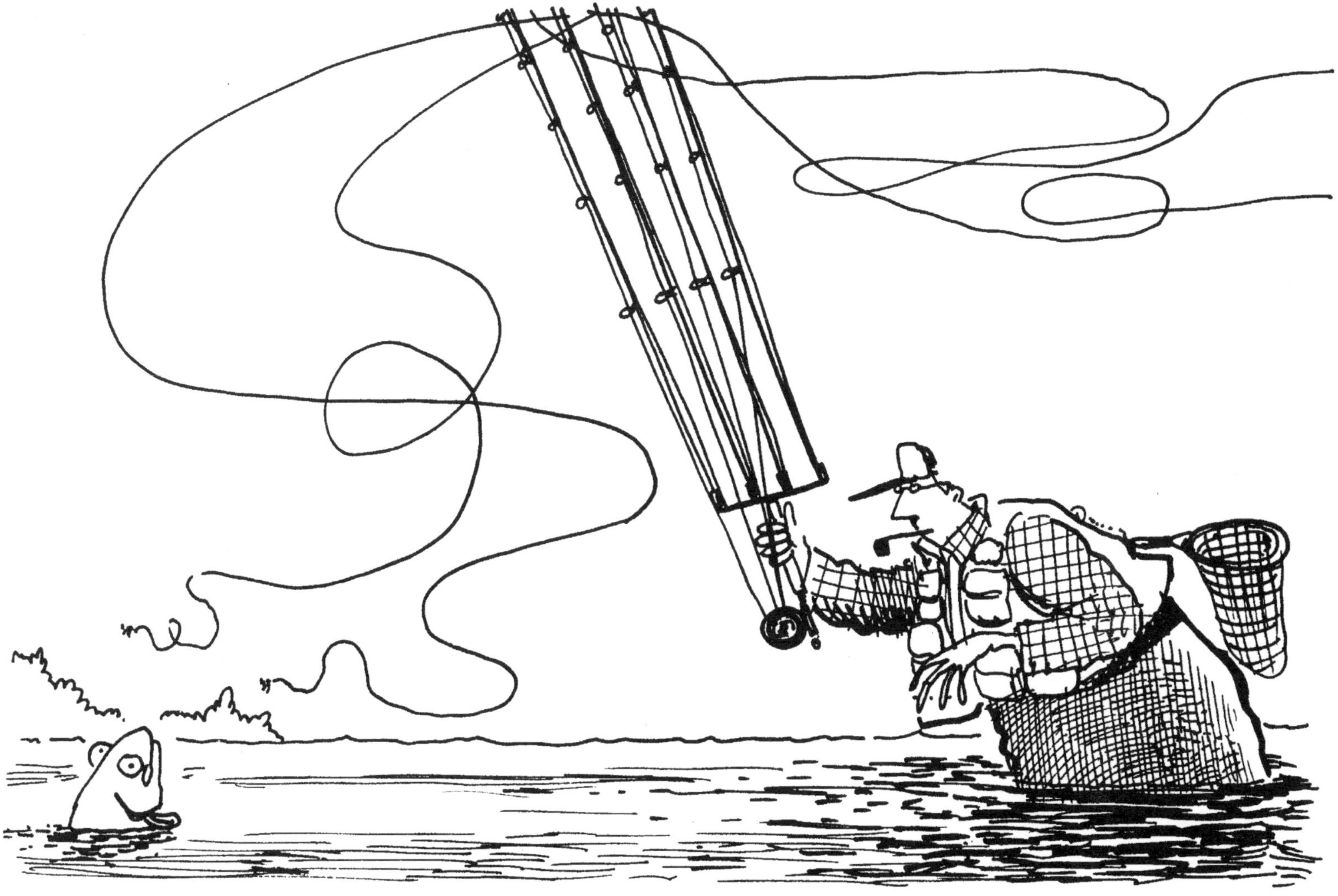

HEINRICH HIMMLER FLY CASTING SCHOOL

Want to learn how to cast? Learn the hard way at the Heinrich Himmler Fly Casting School. You'll receive instruction from the meanest staff assembled since the Second World War. Relentless, unforgiving bastards who all have Argentine citizenship will show you the basics of fly casting. You will learn to fly cast — they have ways of making you load, double haul, and keep your arm at ten and two. It's very simple . . . if you follow orders. Class duration: three years, with time off for good behavior. May not be legal in states that observe the Geneva Convention.

Price 6000000 deutsche marks (gold bullion also acceptable).

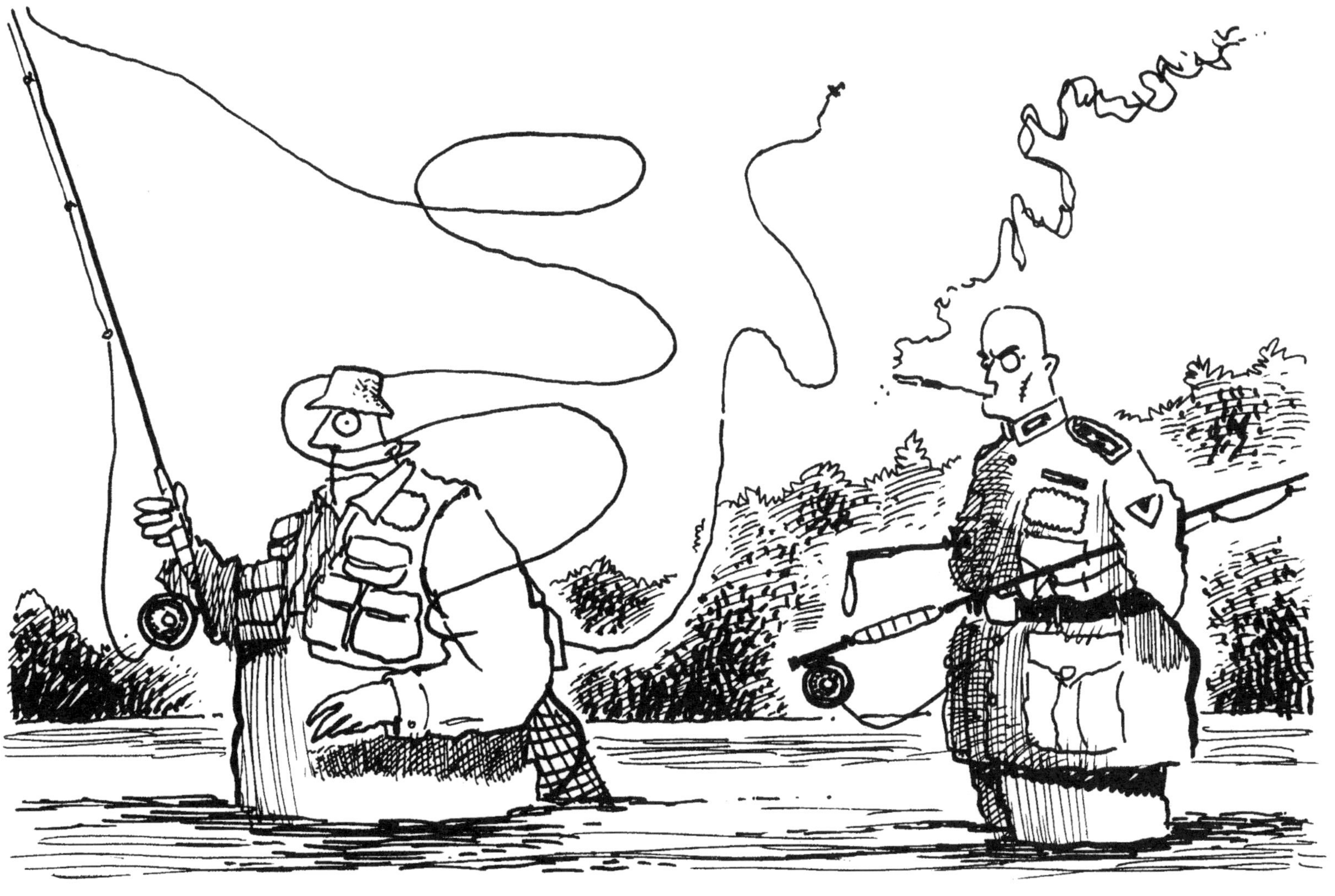

STEALTH MATERIAL WADER®

What's more important than sneaking up on a pod of rising trout? Blending in with your environment is crucial. And what better way to blend in than with patented Stealth technology? You'll love the Stealth waders from CasperTek. Made from the same composite polymers as the F117 bomber, the stealthwader provides instant cover. If you're not there, they don't see you.

Colors: Invisible.
Price: Classified.

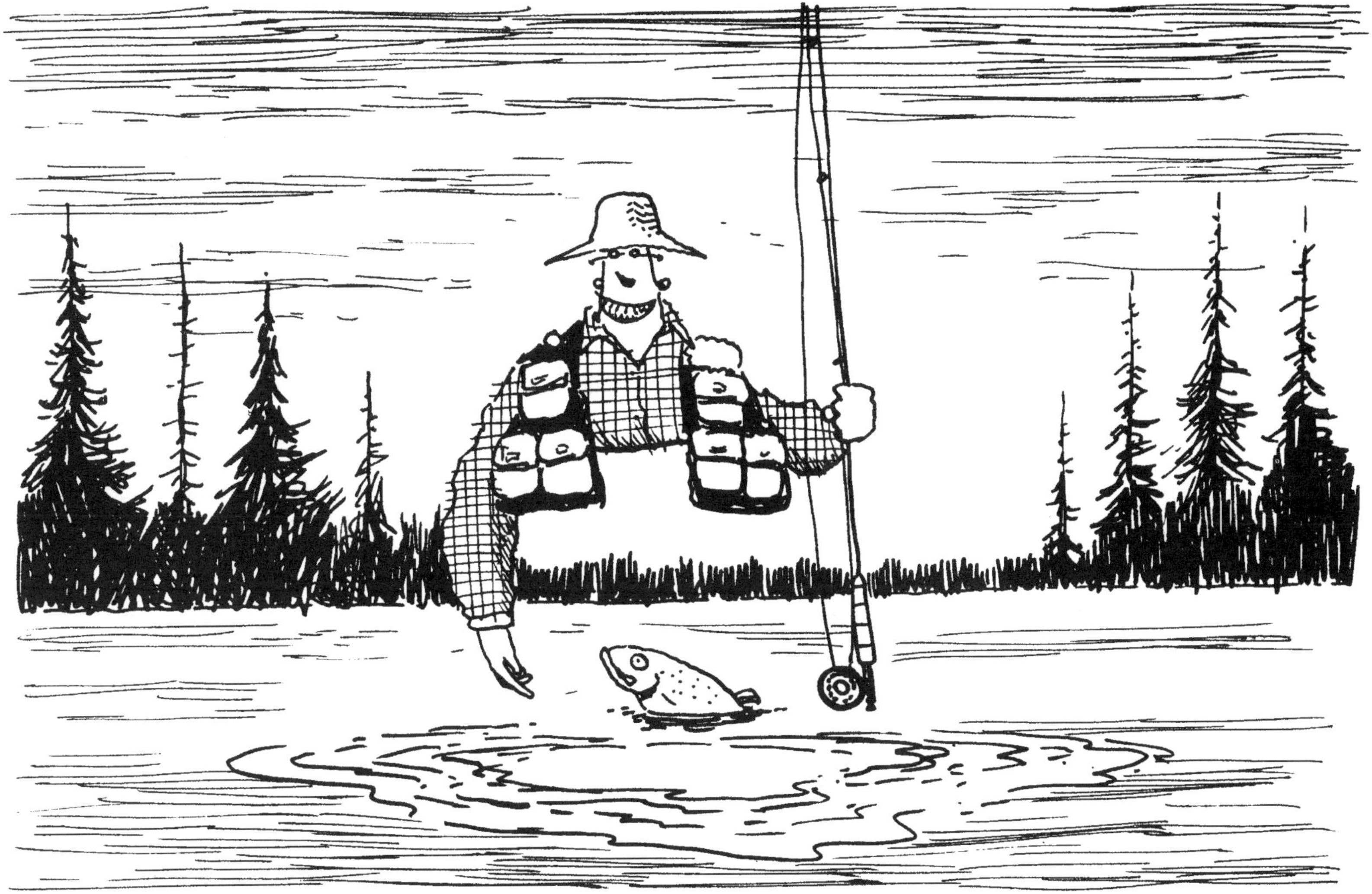

FILE-A-VEST®

How many times have you found that you're short a pocket on your vest? Who hasn't? There's never enough space for the sixty extra spools of 8x, or the sixteen back-up zingers, or the fly box filled entirely with size 24 cream midges. That's why there's the File-a-Vest®, from Disorganization Technologies. With File-a-Vest®, there's always room for what others may consider "superfluous" stuff; but you know better. Who knows when you're going to need that spool full of DT-2-F or the bamboo rod making kit at streamside? With over 1,670 separate pockets, File-a-Vest® makes a slightly weighty but stylish fashion/fishin' statement, and keeps your stash of size 28 midge hooks from getting mixed up with your inflatable dinghy.

Colors: Harvest Gold, Avocado Green, Teal, Puce, Camouflage, Chartreuse.
Price: $560.95.

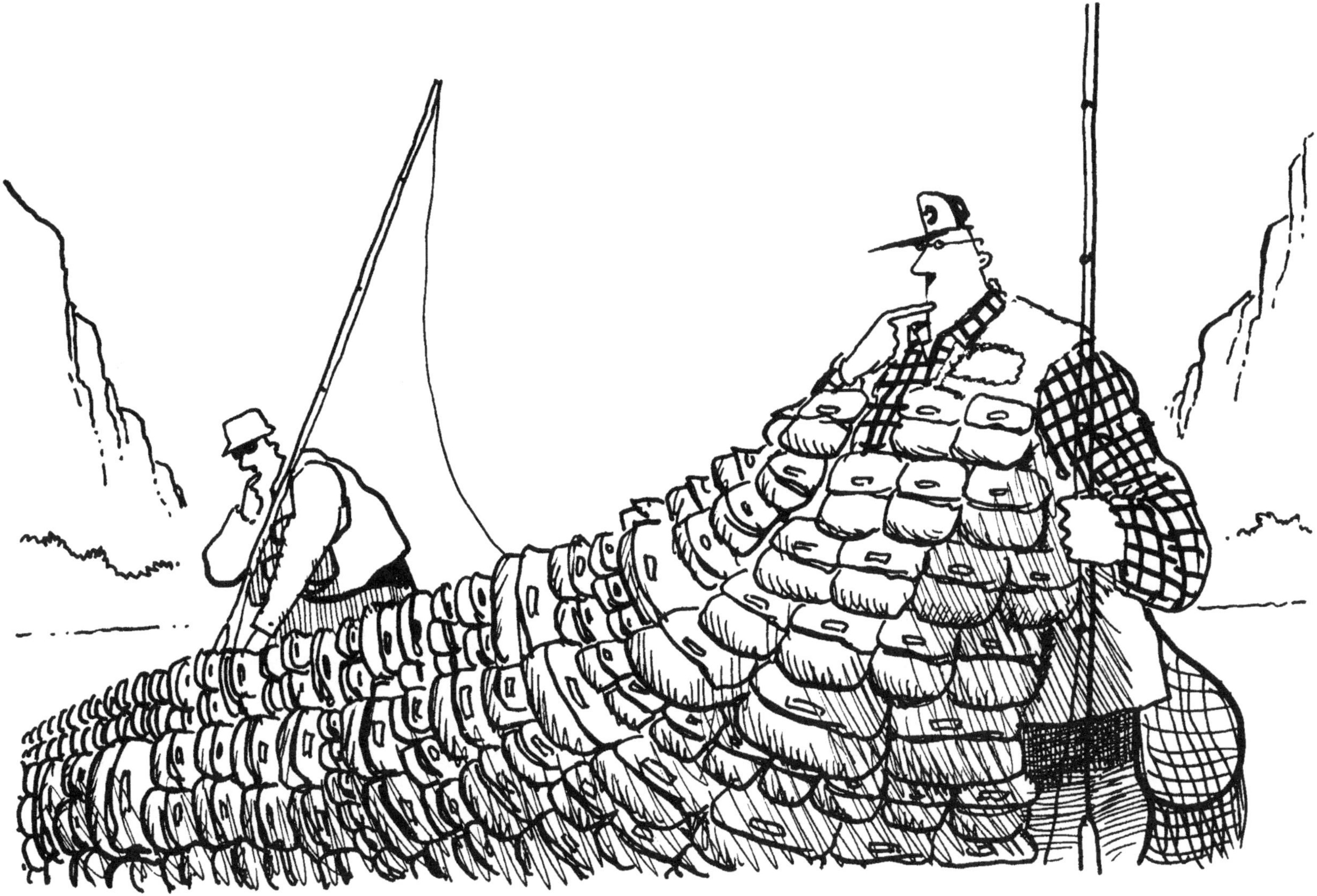

THE BETTY FORD CENTER
FOR FLY FISHING DEPENDENCY

Honest, honey, I can stop fly fishing anytime I want." How many times have we said those words to our abandoned loved ones? A thousand times? A million times? If you really want to get your fly fishing back to sensible levels, you'll need more than professional help . . . you need the former First Lady of the United States. The Betty Ford Center for Fly Fishing Dependency is located in Rancho Orvis, California, and will take you on the 12 steps of recovery to fly fishing sanity. This is not a cold turkey, quit-fly fishing program . . . it's the path back to normal levels of fly fishing; say, fifty times per year. Trained, compassionate staffers, all of whom were fly fishing junkies who broke out into cold sweat if their copy of the latest Orvis catalog was fifteen minutes late, will help you find a balance. The six-month stay includes long periods of not fishing (up to two days in some dire cases) and long walks with an unstrung rod.

Price: $67,000 per week. Includes straitjacket with a fleece patch.

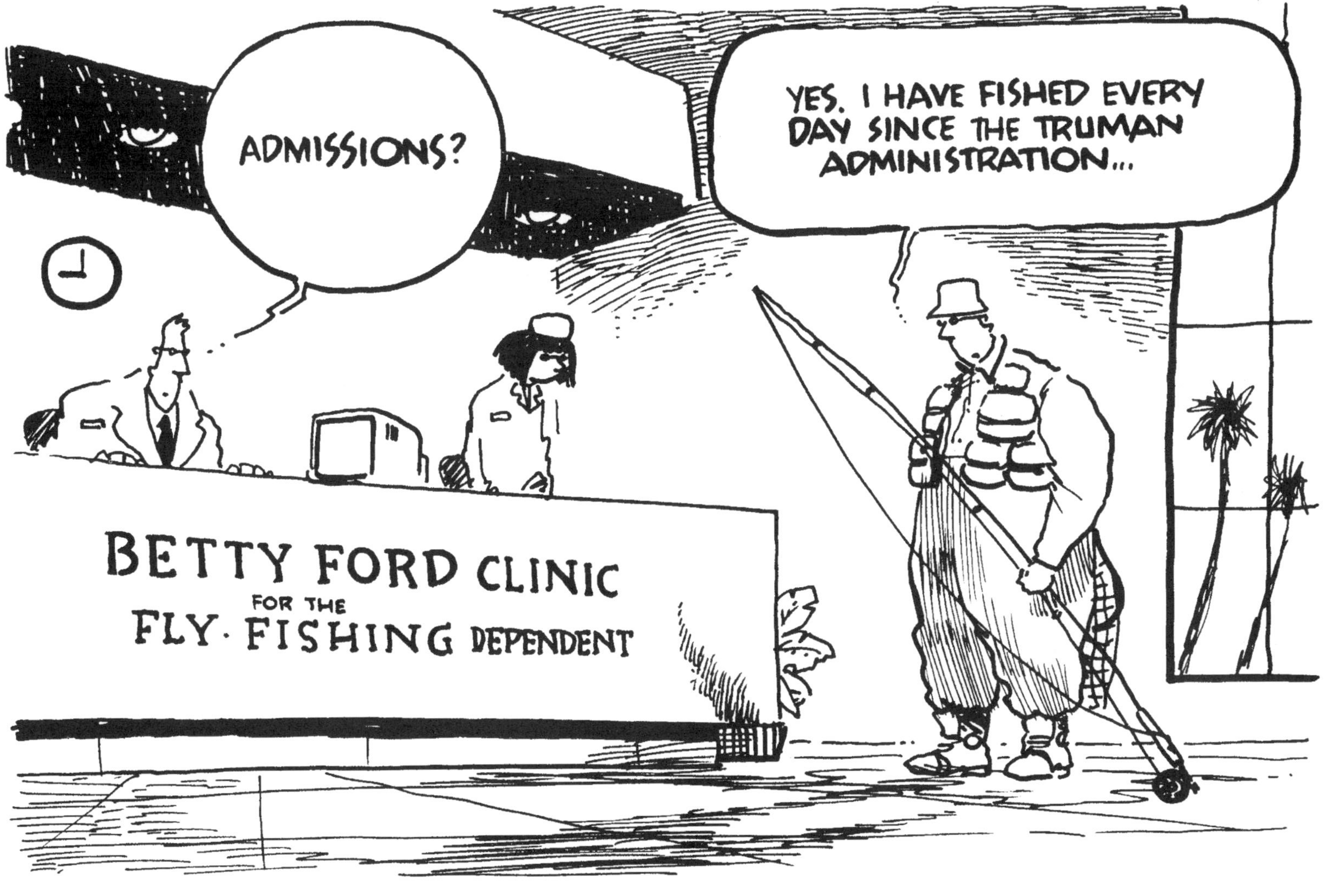
ADMISSIONS?
YES. I HAVE FISHED EVERY DAY SINCE THE TRUMAN ADMINISTRATION...
BETTY FORD CLINIC FOR THE FLY·FISHING DEPENDENT

HOOKED ON TROUT PHONICS®

Do you ever wonder how trout communicate? How do they tell each other that the caddis hatch is on, and only take the size 16s? Language experts at the Defense Language Institute at Monterrey, California, have discovered the secret: the Trout Language! Until last year, no man knew the secret of trout communication. Now it's available to you in a series of eight two-hour instructional tapes. Hooked on Trout Phonics® will have you communicating effortlessly with the big boys at the bottom of the pool in no time. Easier than Russian, but slightly more difficult than French,

Hooked on Trout Phonics® teaches you the trout declensions, and their secret language rules that will have you eavesdropping on what the larger specimens are taking. Here's a sample:

TROUT LANGUAGE: "Gren forgentu makbar."
TRANSLATION: "The idiot is using 4x when he should be going to 6x."

Comes with a handsome plastic binder and a trout language thesaurus.
Price: Five easy payments of $13.95.

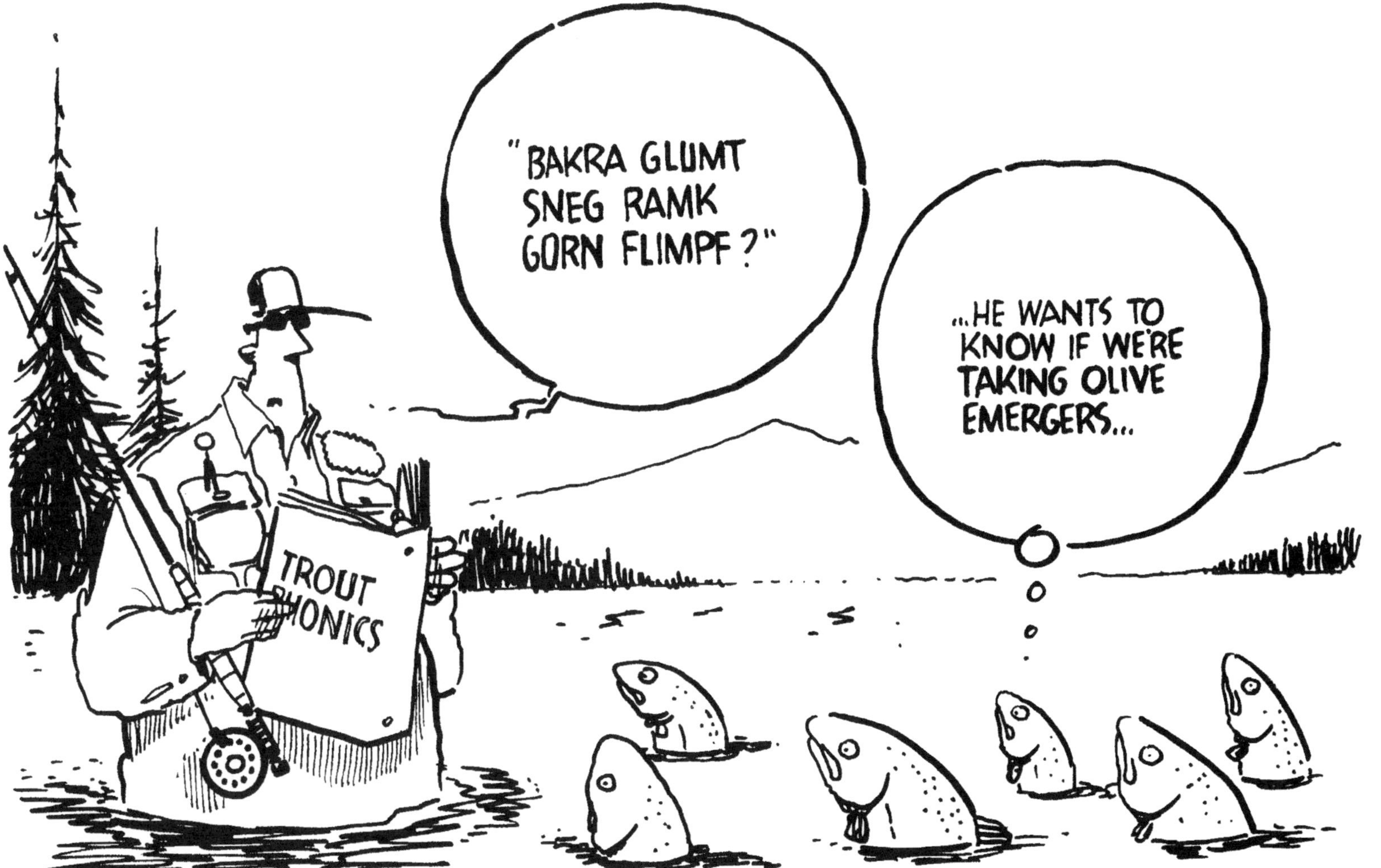
"BAKRA GLUMT SNEG RAMK GORN FLIMPF?"
...HE WANTS TO KNOW IF WE'RE TAKING OLIVE EMERGERS...
TROUT PHONICS

MARTHA STEWART'S TROUT FISHING®

Tired of catching trout in a messy outdoor tableau that won't make the grade with the decorating police. Do you want perfect fly fishing moments that you'll remember long after the cheeseball and marshmallow crowd head back to their poorly decorated double-wides? Then you'll want Martha Stewart's Fishing. Martha Stewart's Fishing® will provide that touch of class to any trout fishing trip. Open the tasteful wicker creel gift basket to find everything you'll need for a total design concept fishing experience. Trout doilies, rainbow trout snugs, English country style flies, reel cozies, vest cachets, and an instruction video featuring Martha Stewart on aesthetically pleasing casting techniques that will make you the most tasteful fisherman around.

Price: $575.99. Available in Streamside Brown, Deep Pool Blue and Mauve Meadow.

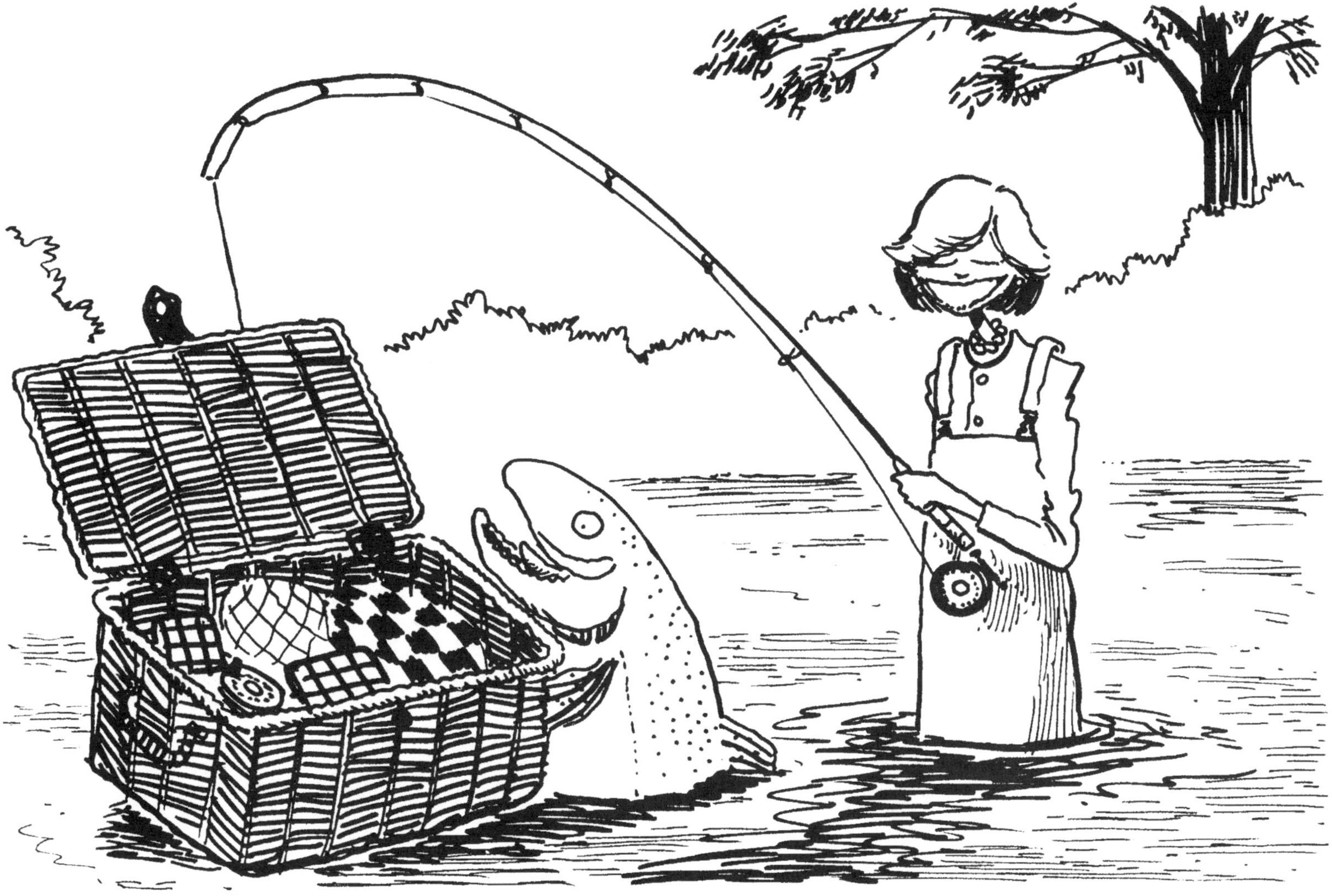

TroutSnax®

Tired of matching the hatch? Absolutely sick about not getting that Masters in entomology? Agonize no more with tender, golden juicy, delicious TroutSnax® from Salmonida Cuisine Styrategies. They've created tasty bite sized chunks of trout dining pleasure that will say "goodbye Baetis, hello bait" before you can say emergent trailing nymphal husk. Just pop on a TroutSnax®, and trout will be fighting to get on your barbless hook. TroutSnax® are available in delicious flavors ranging from Browntrout Bites, Kamloops Parfait, Brookie Pate, Rainbow Whiz, PorkRind Sparkle Pupa, and Grayling Gulps. Available in kosher varieties, too! TroutSnax® — *When cheating meets eating.*

Price: $39.95 per one ounce (resealable bag).

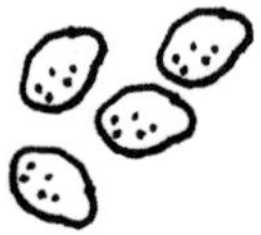

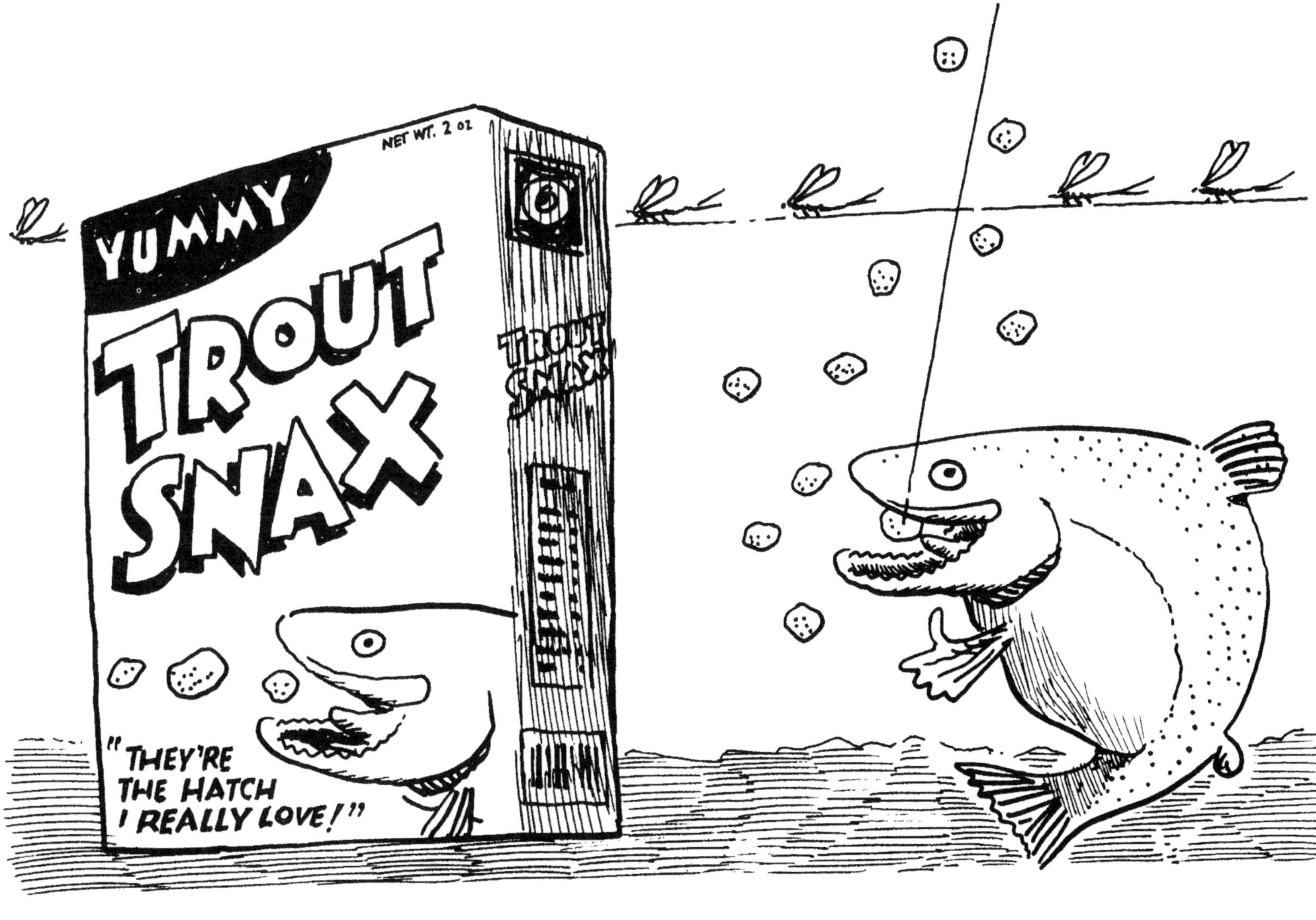
NET WT. 2 oz
YUMMY
TROUT SNAX
"THEY'RE THE HATCH I REALLY LOVE!"
TROUT SNAX

VIRTUAL REALITY TROUT STREAM®

Let's pretend you're really lucky and get to fish twice a month. Over a fifty year period, that's only about 600 times. What do you do to tide yourself over between trips? Thanks to the latest computer technology and the blood, sweat and tears of people you teased in high school, you can fish in the privacy of your own home or office with the Virtual Reality Trout Stream®. Virtual Reality is the computer-created environment that allows you to experience an illusion as if it was an actual event. Of course, it isn't, but you could say that about most of your trout fishing trips. With the Virtual Reality Trout Stream®, you don the special Virtual Reality Trout Stream Suit® and take hold of the Virtually Real Trout Rod sensor unit®, program your river software (over 140 to choose from, including Henry's Fork, the Yellowstone, The Frying Pan, The Beaverkill, the Neversink, and dozens of other famous streams), and let your computer-generated double haul fly! Thrill to high-res pixel browns taking fly after fly, or increase the skill level and punch in the selectivity level you want! It's all here! Glassy slicks, fast riffles, pocket water — all with the flick of a chip. Don't worry about falling in, either, although standing in a bathtub increases the sensory illusion (not to mention the risk of fatal shock). Get Virtually Real today!

Price: $56,000 (equal to three fully guided days in New Zealand).

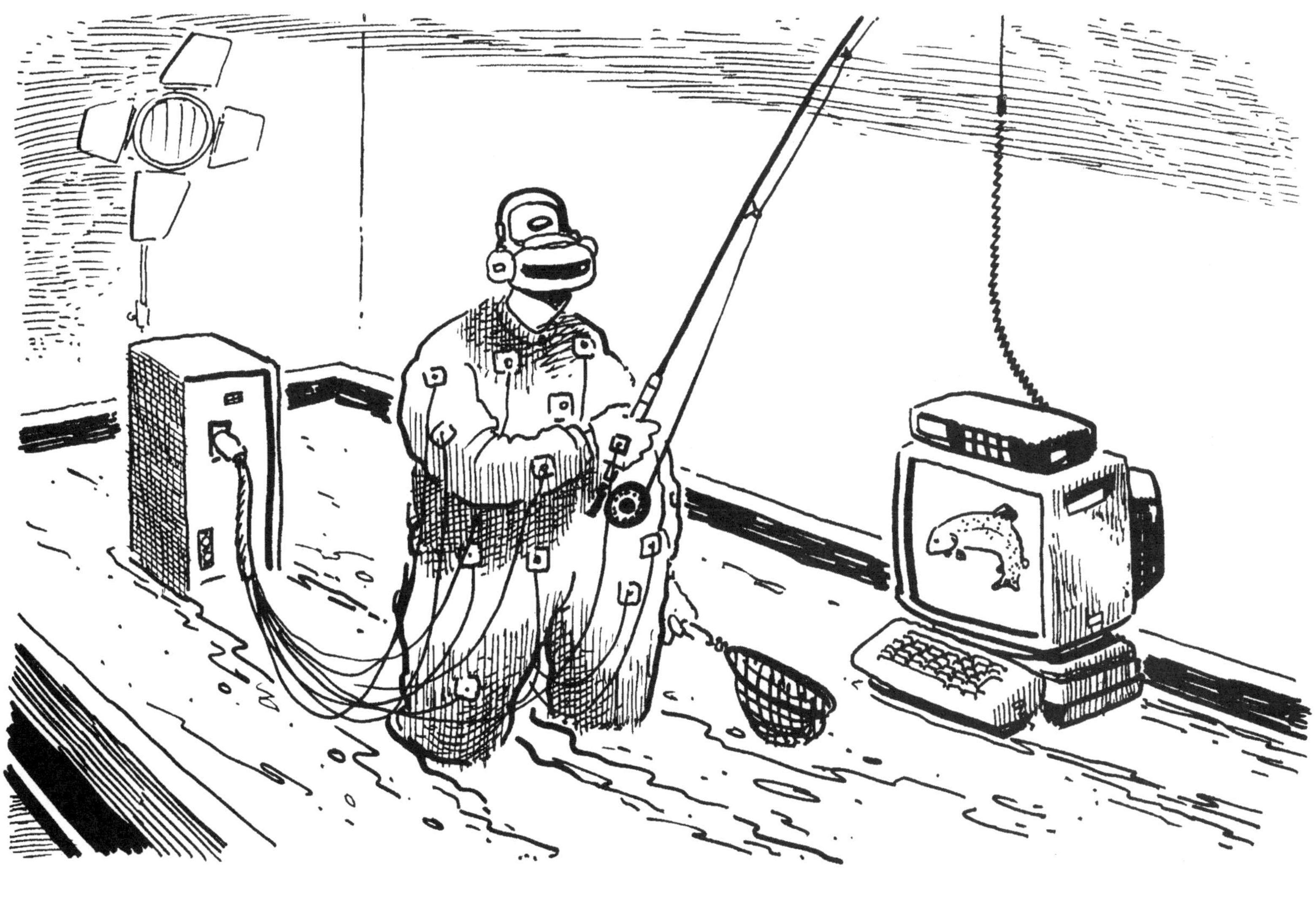

THE FLY ROD CONDO®

First there was the fly rod aluminum tube. Then came the fly rod zipper case. Now there's the ultimate fly rod storage idea: The Fly Rod Condo®. Pamper your rods with the Fly Rod Condo®. The Fly Rod Condo® is a 1600 square foot, two bedroom, two bath, fleece-lined complete storage system for your precious fly rods. The Fly Rod Condo® can store up to six thousand fly rods, with all the comforts of home! Microwave oven, hot tub, and a moisture-free environment add up to the best fly rod storage yet. You can even visit with your fly rods — stay overnight if you like!

Colors: Consult with contractor.
Price: $79,500.00, 10.65% fixed rate mortgage, 7% real estate broker's fee.

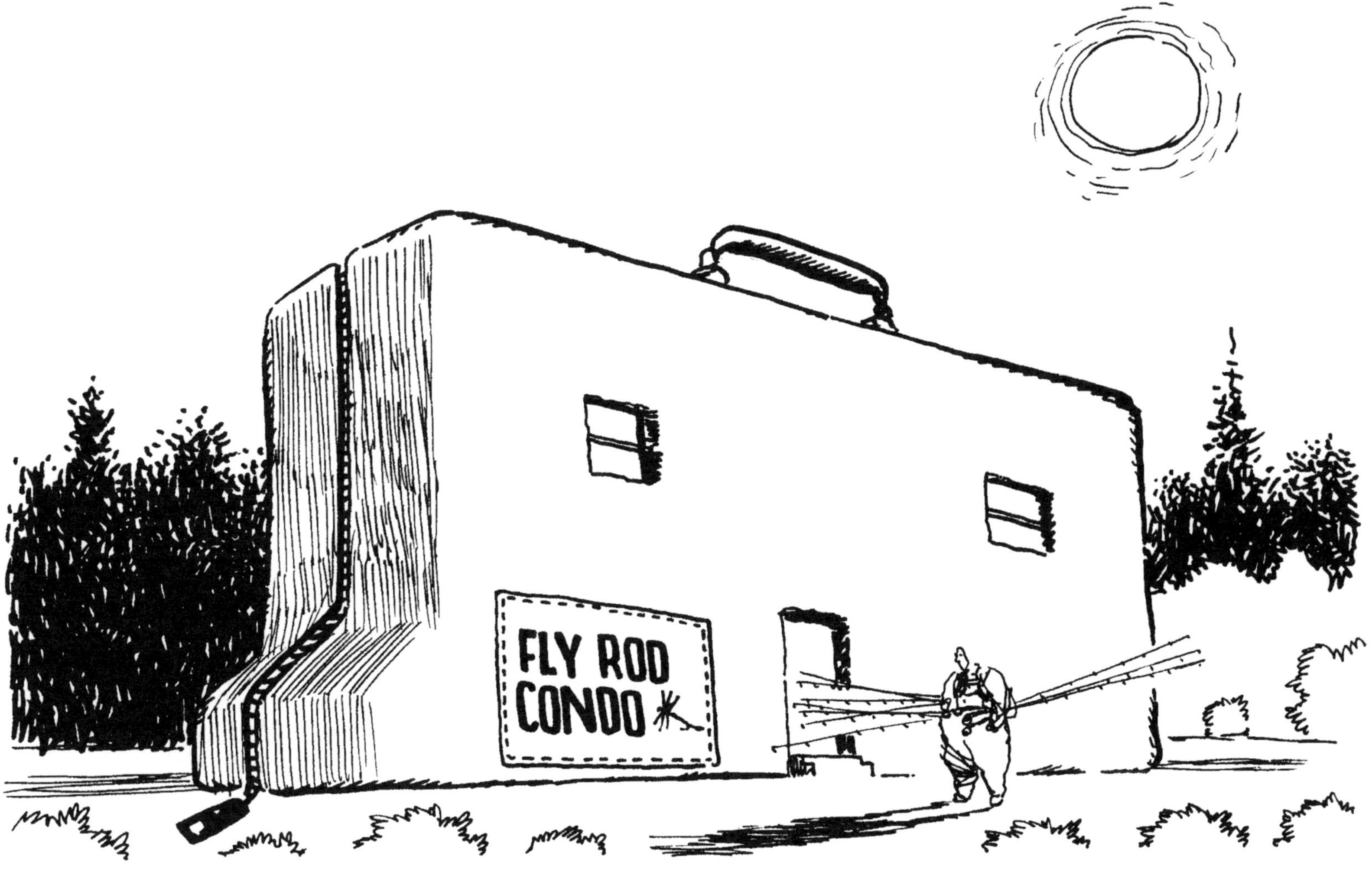
FLY ROD
CONDO

THE PRE-TANGLED LEADER®

When you go to put on a new leader, you don't want any surprises or guesswork. You'll want to know that when you open that leader package during the big hatch, it will be reliably and hopelessly tangled. You don't want the guesswork that goes with ripping open the package and wondering whether that leader is going to be usable, as it is about 40% of the time with regular leaders. With the Pre-tangled Leader®, you know it's screwed up, from the butt to the tippet, eliminating any frustration trying to untangle it when the pressure's on. Harbor no future illusions about whether your leader works; with the Pre-tangled Leader®, you know it's a goddam mess, first time, every time. The Pre-tangled Leader®: shouldn't you be able to count on something during your fishing trip?

Price: $3 per leader.

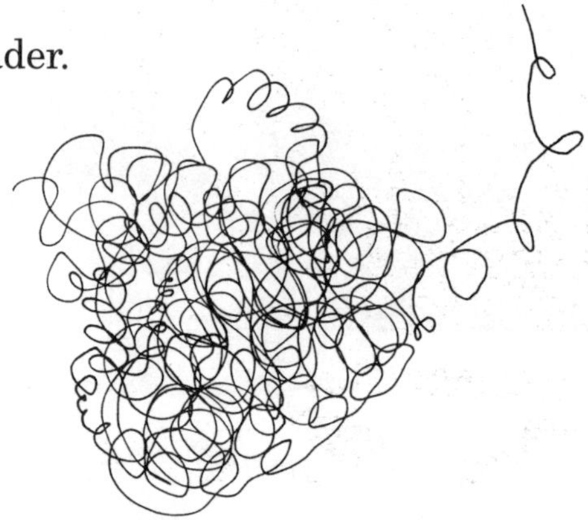

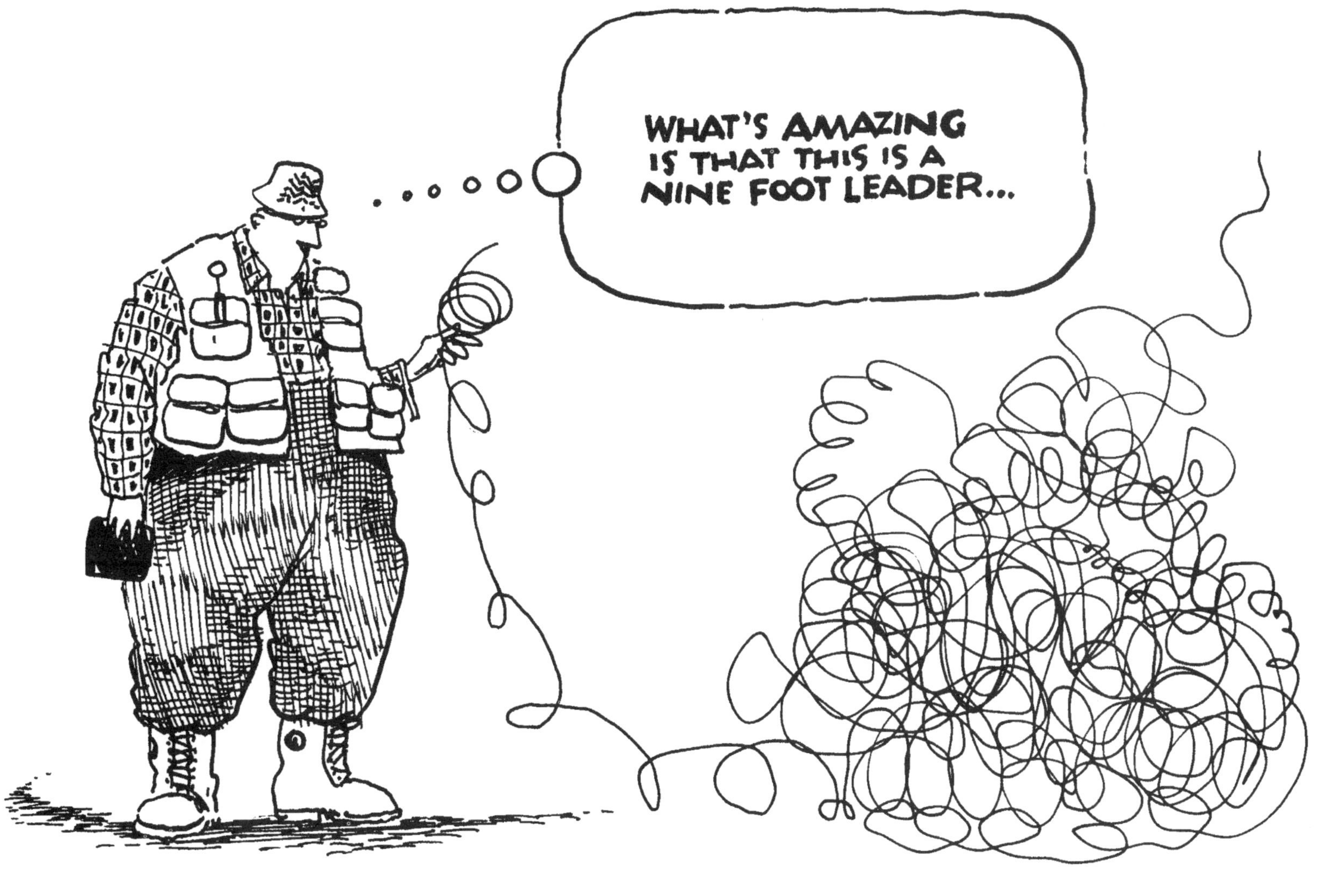
WHAT'S AMAZING IS THAT THIS IS A NINE FOOT LEADER...

TROUT GOOP®

This is an all-purpose, almost indescribably revolting mucilaginous substance that you can smear on anything: lines, leaders, reel gears, sunglasses, rods, fishing partners, even sandwiches! The fact is, no one knows what this stuff is. Our product field testers have analyzed it, and claim its components are slug slime, hand lotion, 10W40 motor oil, library paste, rendered farm animals, and New Jersey topsoil. Yuck! On the other hand, who knows what's in fly floatant?

Color: Glop.
Price: $4 per 80 gallon drum.

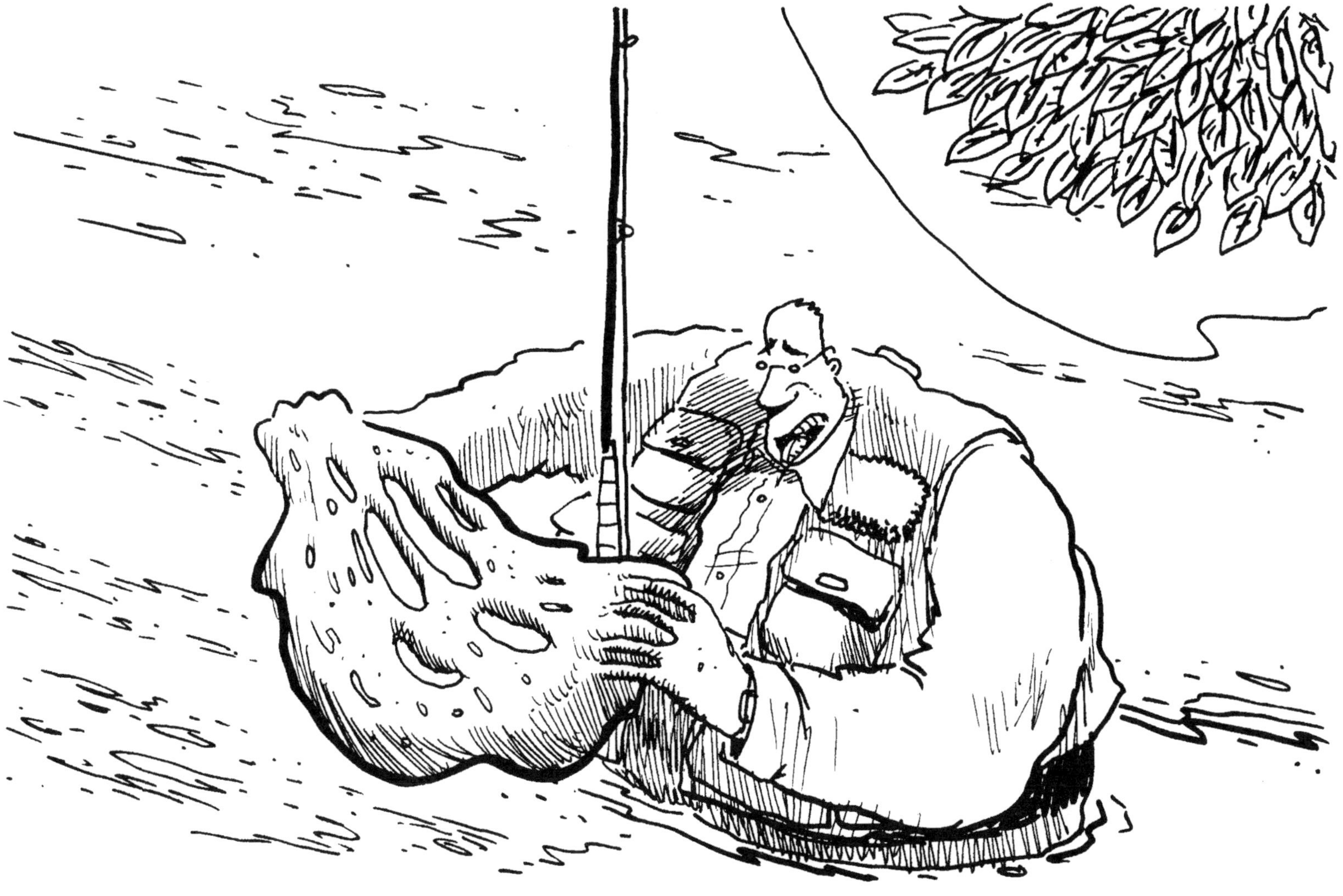

FLY FISHING LITERARY SOCIETY BOOK CLUB

Join the Fly Fisherman's Literary Society Book Club and read up on the hot new trends, literary ruminations of the angling elite, and instructional books that will help you to become even more obscure to your regular friends, if you have any left at this point. This month's seletions:

The Unabobber by Agents of the Federal Bureau of Investigation. This fast-paced action-packed thriller takes you on the nationwide manhunt for the man who serially fished bait on all of the catch-and-release blue ribbon trout waters for the last twenty years. Read excerpts from *The Unabobber's Manifesto*, decrying the elitist snob fly fishing elite that tied up much of the great dry fly water of the country with its Big Brother fishing regulations. $19.95.

The Emergent Trailing Nymphal Husk by Gary Boring. Top rod Gary Boring takes you step by step through 565 pages of how to recognize, tie, and fish this most intriguing of hatches. Includes 90 pages of color plates, 120 pages of entomological history of the insect and its phenomenon, and over 300 pages of math problems. $39.95.

The Fly Fishing History of World War II by Stephen Ambrose. Join Ike, Patton, MacArthur and Bradley as they fly fish their way to victory over the Axis powers. Discover newly released documents that reveal Hitler's race to discover graphite, and the Japanese master plan to corner the bamboo market. $24.95.

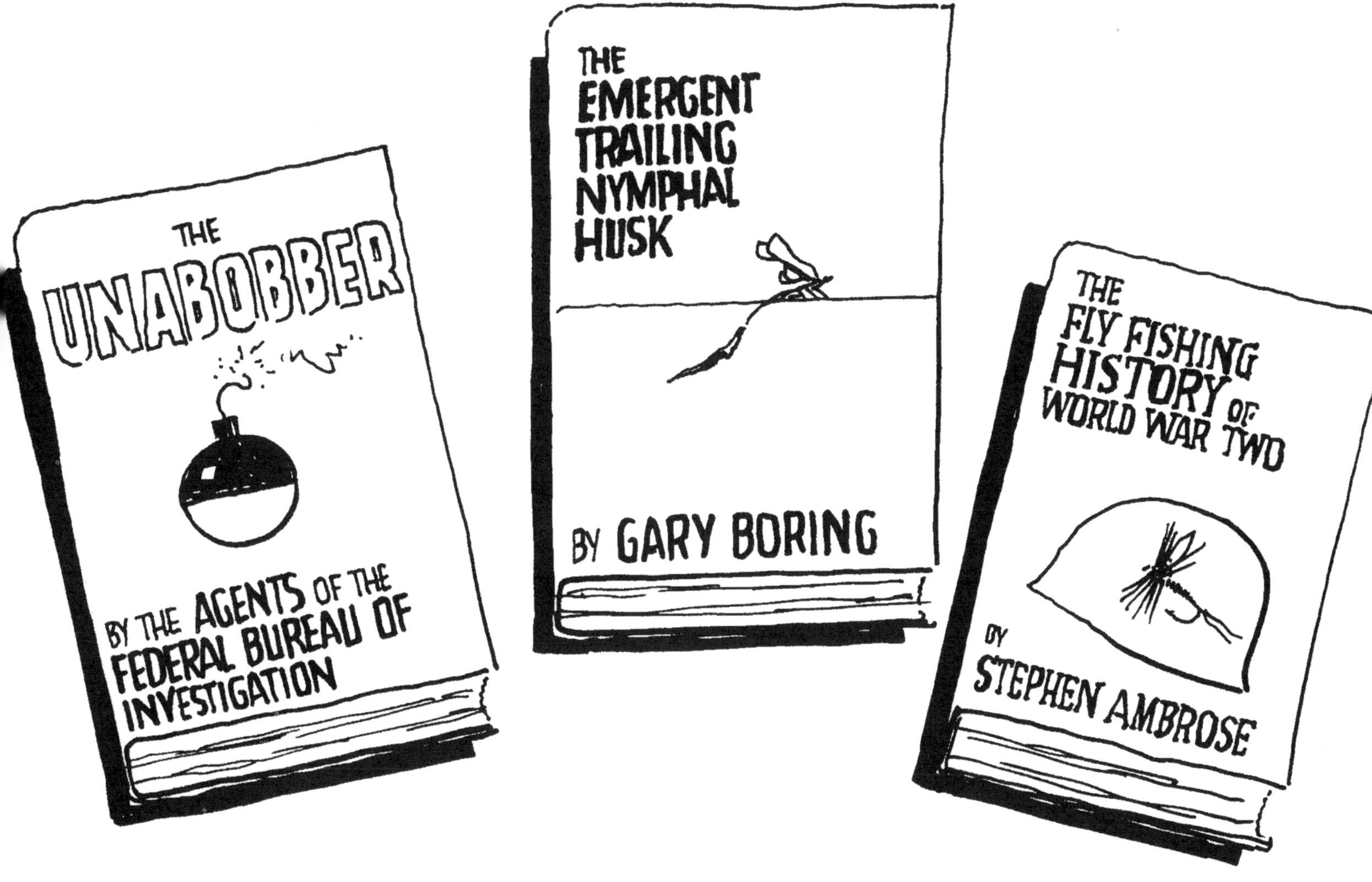
THE UNABOBBER
BY THE AGENTS OF THE FEDERAL BUREAU OF INVESTIGATION
THE EMERGENT TRAILING NYMPHAL HUSK
BY GARY BORING
THE FLY FISHING HISTORY OF WORLD WAR TWO
BY STEPHEN AMBROSE

OUTFIT YOURSELF FOR UNDER $20®

Do you want to start fly fishing, but are put off by the seemingly prohibitive price tag? Fret no more with this serviceable starter outfit. Glad bag waders (3 mils thick!); all-aluminum car aerial rod (it's even collapsible); high quality Campbell's Soup tin can reel — with a genuine handle (like the pros use!); strong, durable twineline; grocery bag vest with real armholes, and assortment of two flies.

Price: $19.99.

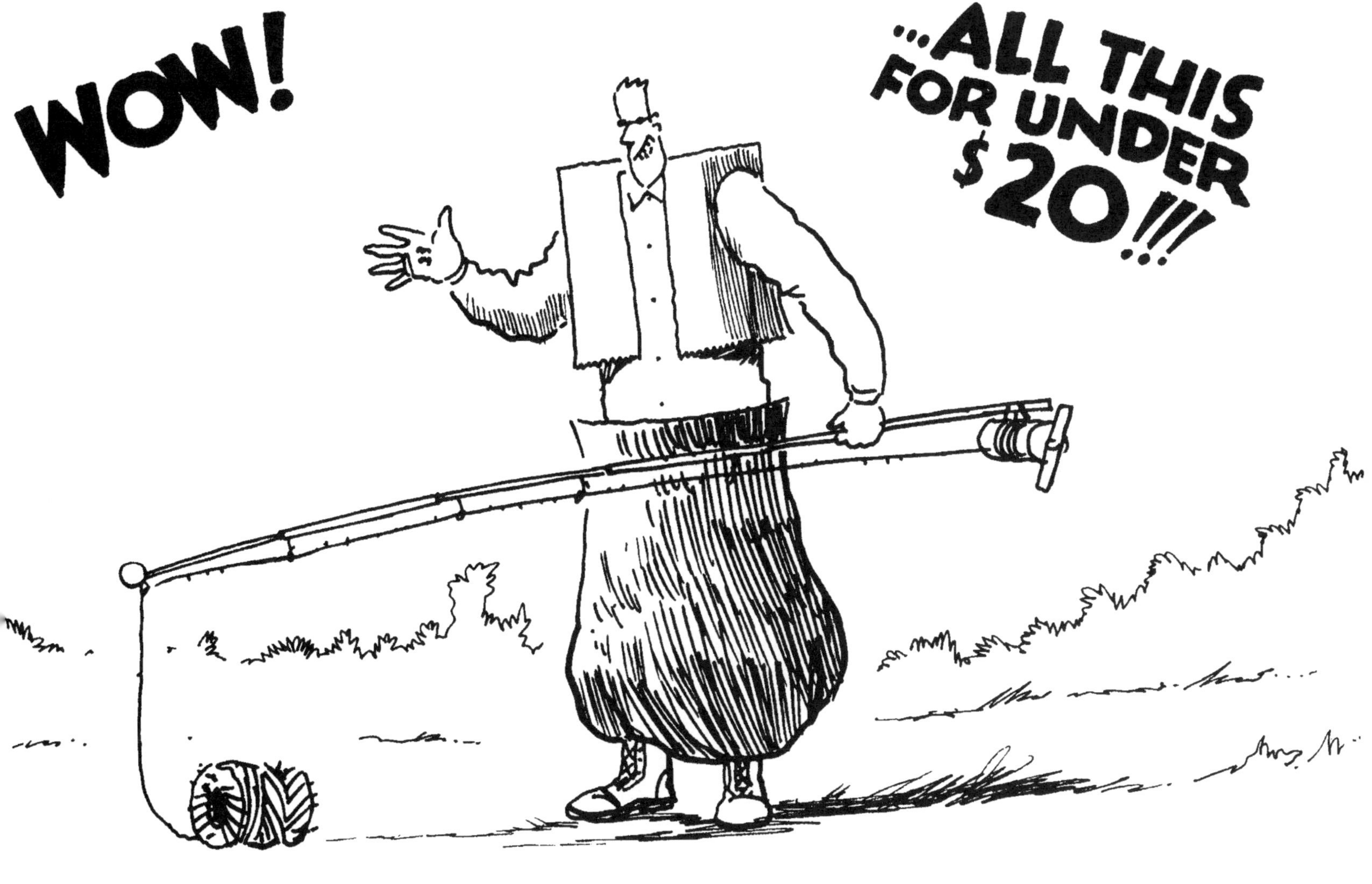
WOW!
...ALL THIS FOR UNDER $20!!!

THE VERY, *VERY* BRITISH FLY BOX®

What's classier than anything British? A piece of British technology that doesn't work, that's what. With the very, very British Fly Box®, you'll get a terribly attractive, almost perfectly non-functioning piece of technology that never, ever works properly. Go ahead — try to open up one of the twenty tiny windows that contain the fly you so desperately need when the Hendrickson are floating and the trout are in a feeding frenzy. It won't open. Shake it, pound it with a rock, shoot its little latch with a .30/06 rifle: it still won't open. But you know when that hatch is over, that latch will spring open randomly and let all your flies out and you'll watch them float downstream, gobbled up by the trout you couldn't attract. But imagine all the admiring comments you'll receive when your snob fishing buddies see you struggling against the odds to open it.

Price: $395, or 680£.

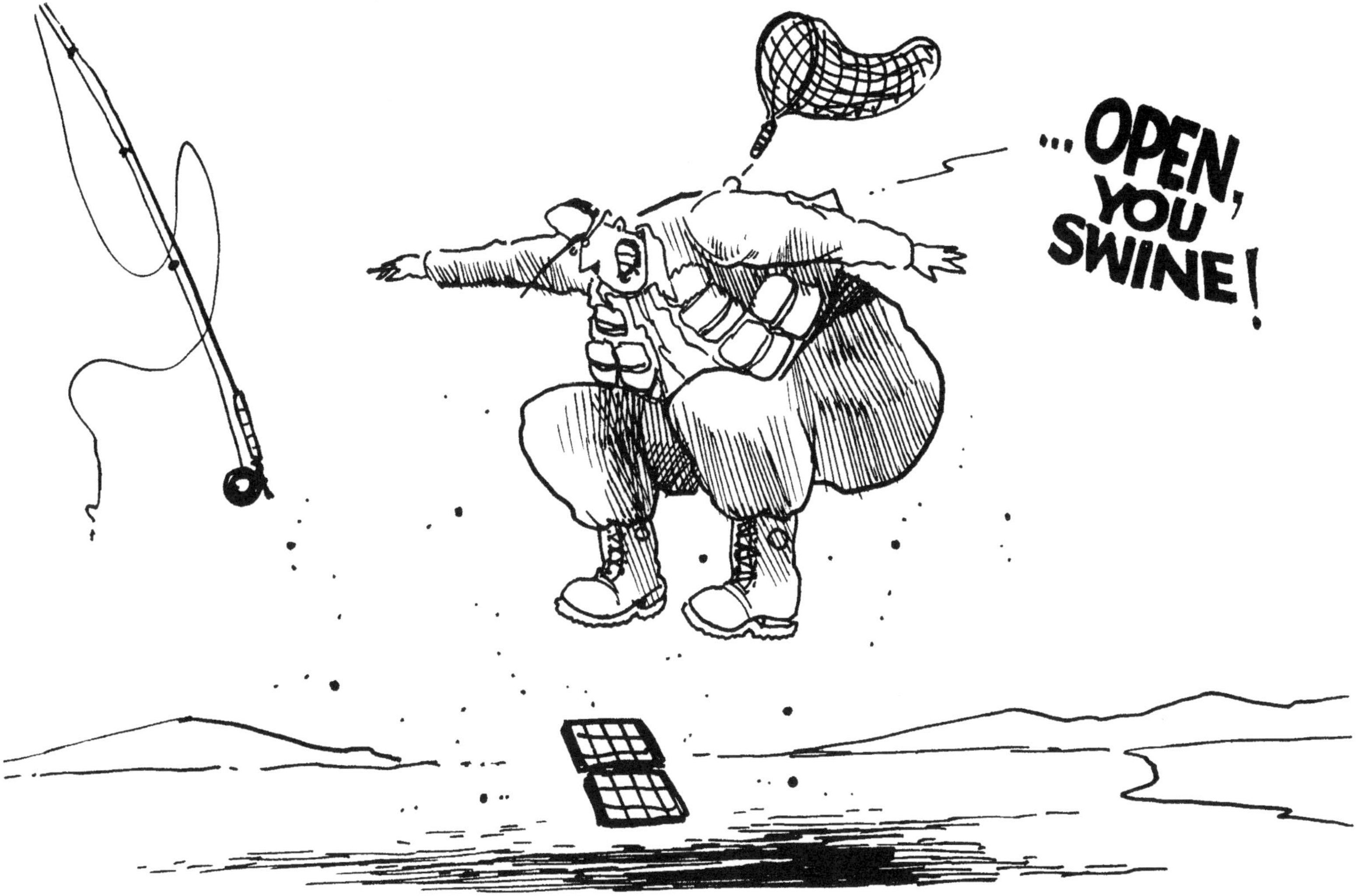
...OPEN, YOU SWINE!

TROUT GUM®

When you can't trout fish, chew Trout Gum®. Made from real trout parts by Wriggly Gum Company. Tastes like the real thing. Pure trout chewing satisfaction means you'll have a minty/trouty taste in your mouth for hours, even days later. Maintain a distance of fifty feet from unsuspecting humans.

Rainbow and brown flavors only.
Price: fifty cents per pack.

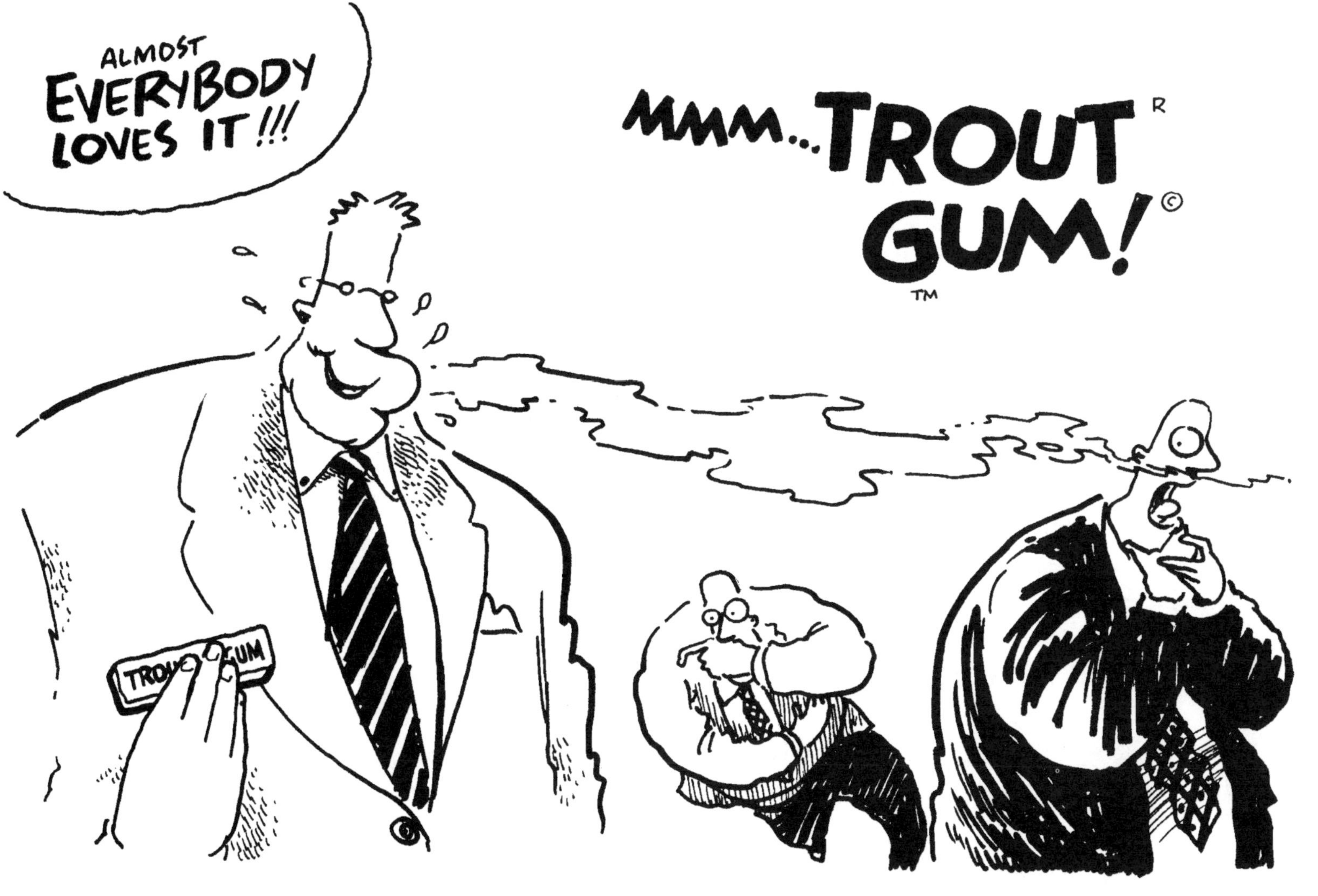
ALMOST EVERYBODY LOVES IT!!!
MMM...TROUT® GUM!©™
TROUT GUM

THE FLY FISHING VIDEO LIBRARY®

The Fly Fishing Video Library offers the finest in fly fishing video instruction and entertainment. Join today and pop in the tapes we're offering this month:

Fly Fishing the Oprah Winfrey Way. Join Oprah as she takes you through her personal struggle to overcome her fly fishing demons. She'll show you how she learned to double haul after years of wimpy fifteen foot casts, how she became a proficient fly tier after her personal fly fishing trainer said it couldn't be done, and how she resisted the temptation to eat her catch live on the banks of the stream. $19.99.

Dan Rather's Fly Fishing Manhattan. Hook up with the CBS News anchor and fish the challenging waters of Midtown Manhattan. Casting for brookies in the ponds of Central Park, brown trout angling in the Hudson (be careful not to hook that mob stoolie), and nymphing for rats in the treacherous New York City sewer system. A special guest appearance by Walter Cronkite tells you about NASA's 1960s contribution to today's hi-tech fly fishing. Dan's friend Kenneth will tell you the frequency of how often you should fish the Big Apple. $21.50.

Del Bottomfieder's Fly Fishing for Carp Videorama. Join host Del Bottomfieder for wacky carp fishing antics as he takes carp after carp on Light Hendricksons. Did you know carp will take a number 2 pencil fished in the surface film? How about carp sucking down emergers in between their usual fare of 10W30 motor oil and coffee cans? It's all here. Carp on! $22.95.

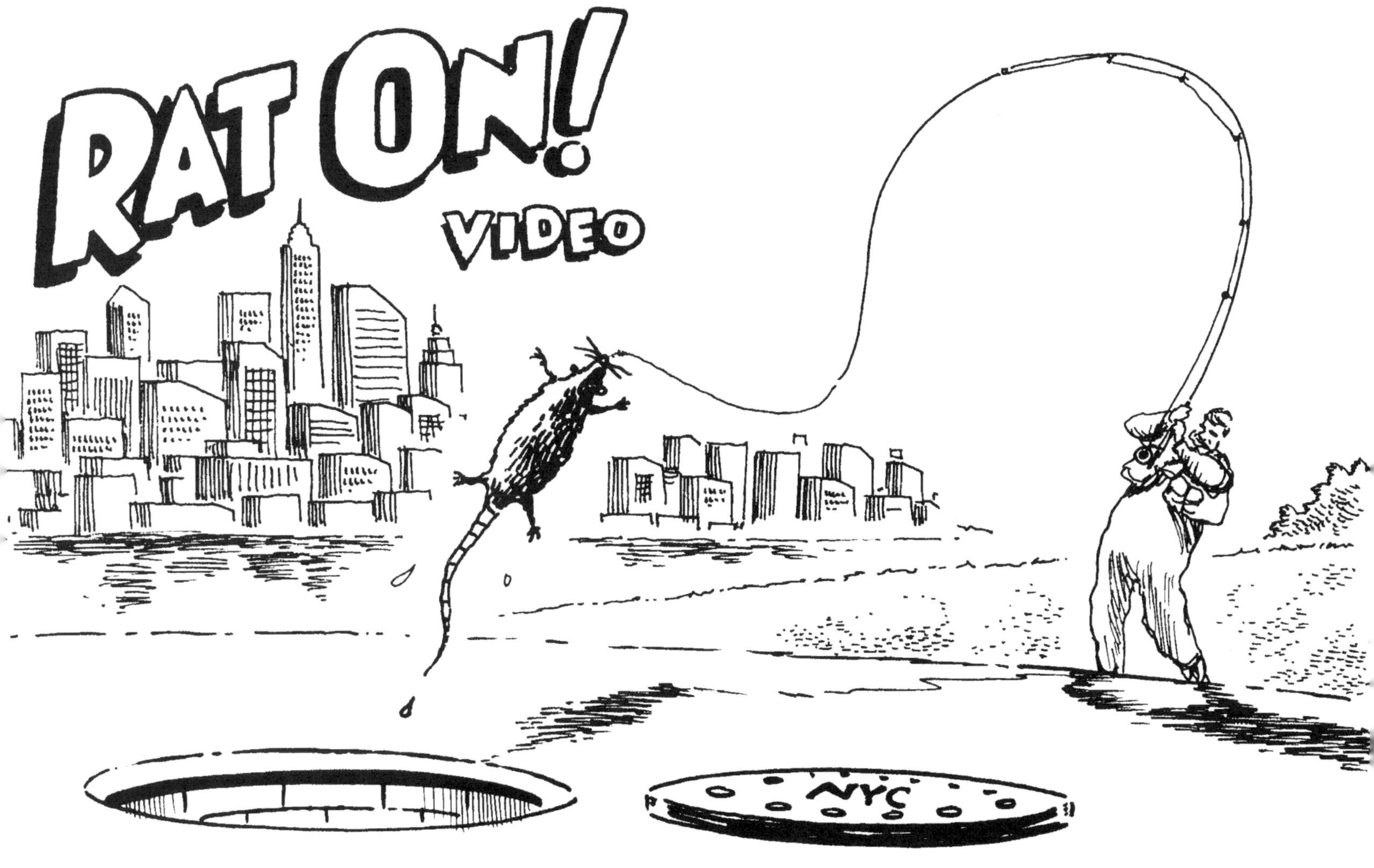
RAT ON!
VIDEO
NYC

PC FLY FISHING LAPTOP®

You've had a hard week at work, hammering away on your PC laptop, crunching numbers that make the defense budget look like your kid's allowance. You're looking forward to a weekend of fly fishing, but don't leave the fun of personal computing behind. Get the PC Fly Fishing Laptop®. Big Blue has perfected the streamside computing system of the future, and the future is now! The PC Fly Fishing Laptop® contains 32 megs of RAM, and lists the weight and length of every trout in every stream in the United States. There's even special Patagonia or New Zealand software for the traveling angler. Don't just go out and fish: Download 'em! Colors: camouflage, tan, olive, gray. External hard drive vest optional. Do not immerse. Save often.

Price: $3995.

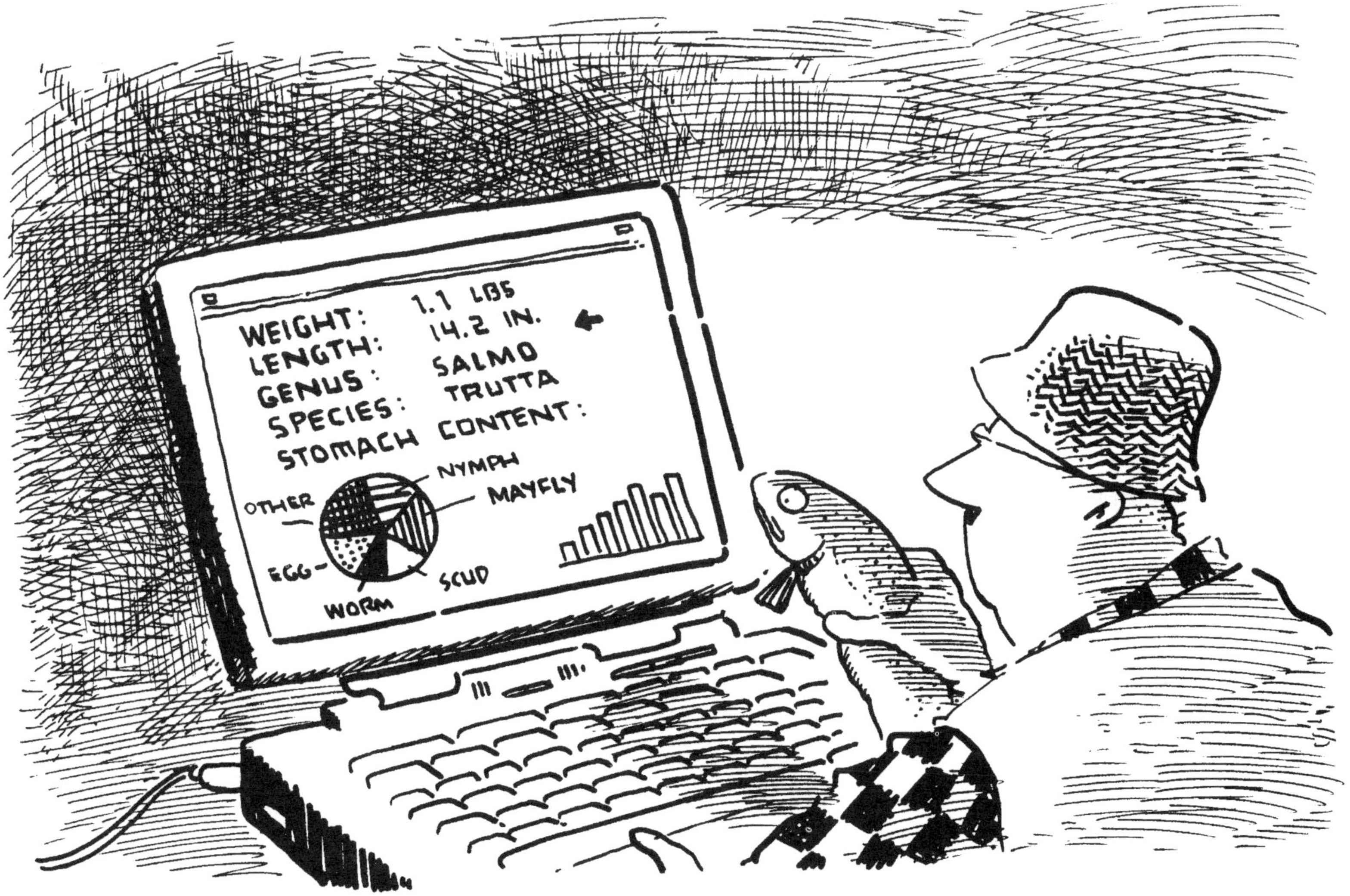
WEIGHT: 1.1 LBS
LENGTH: 14.2 IN.
GENUS: SALMO
SPECIES: TRUTTA
STOMACH CONTENT:
NYMPH
MAYFLY
OTHER
EGG
WORM
SCUD

ZERO G FLY LINE BY SCIENCEFICTION ANGLERS®

Sometimes it seems like dry fly line is a contradiction in terms; your dry fly line never seems to ride high enough. But now with Zero G Fly Line® — it actually flies! Zero G Fly Line® has no weight on earth, no density whatsoever, and is the official fly line of Space Station Freedom! It never touches the water, creating no drag, no splash, and needs no messy fly line dressing. How do they do it? By using UFO sighting technology and a helium core, Zero G Fly Line® makes casting unnecessary — just wad it up in your hand and throw it. But watch out for trees and low-flying aircraft.

Color: infrared, Ultraviolet.
Price: $3.5 million (U.S. Defense Department buyers not eligible for purchase).

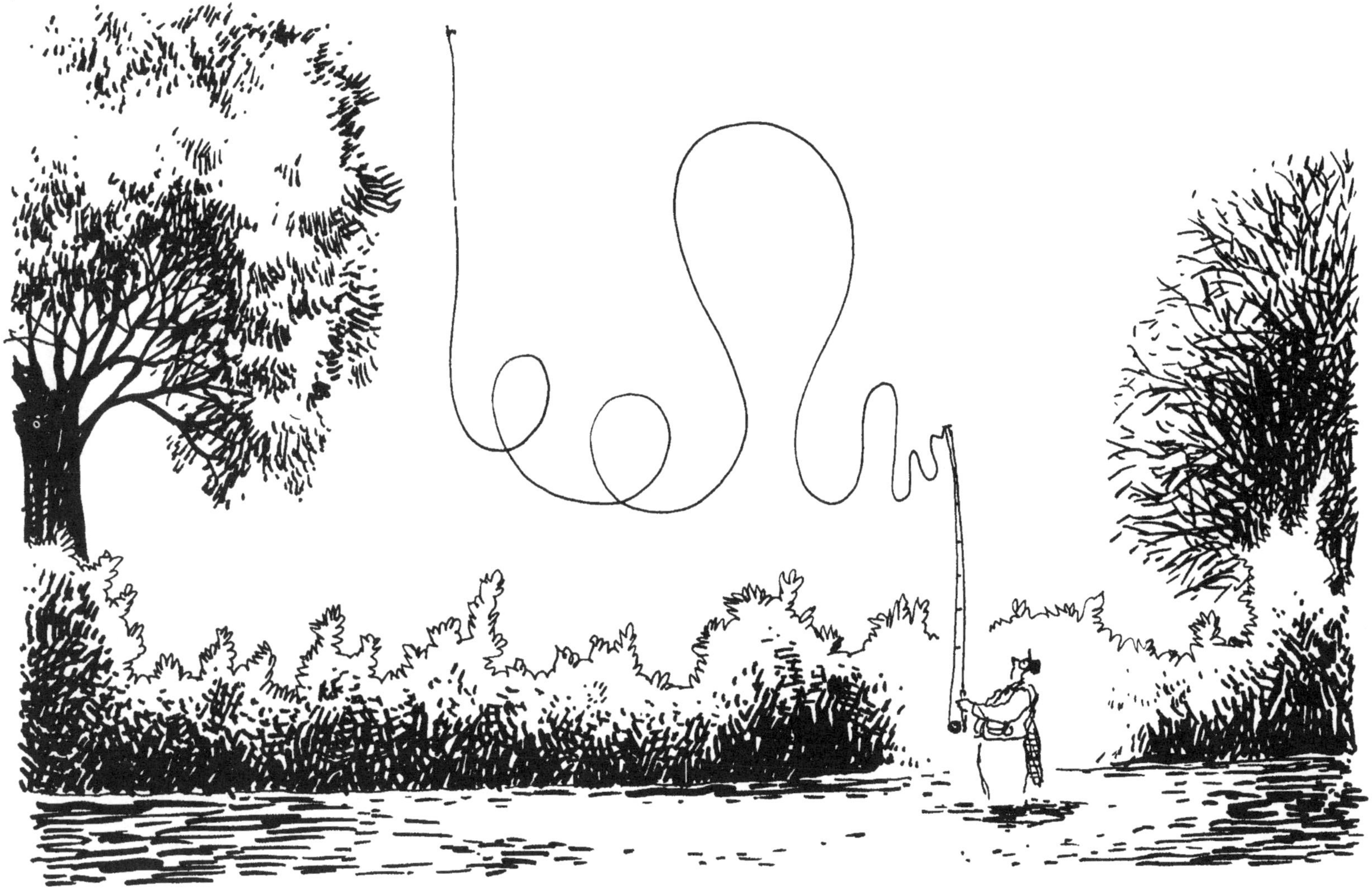

THE CROSS PENROD®

If you're reading this, you're probably a Young Urban Fly Fisherman with the Plutonium American Express Card irradiating your wallet, and a snob to boot. You're probably a traveller who can't take up space in your Hartman overnight bag for a real fly rod, and you appreciate the weight and heft of a truly fine writing instrument. The Cross Penrod® is for you. The Cross Penrod® is both an 8-foot, 5-weight graphite fly rod and a terribly expensive Cross Pen all rolled into one pretentious little package. The Cross Penrod® telescopes into a fast action, slightly inky fly rod that combines the miracle of graphite with the Palmer Method of handwriting. That means great presentation, on the stream and on the stationery.

Color: black, blue. Weight: 1 ounce (without ink or reel).
Price: $350.

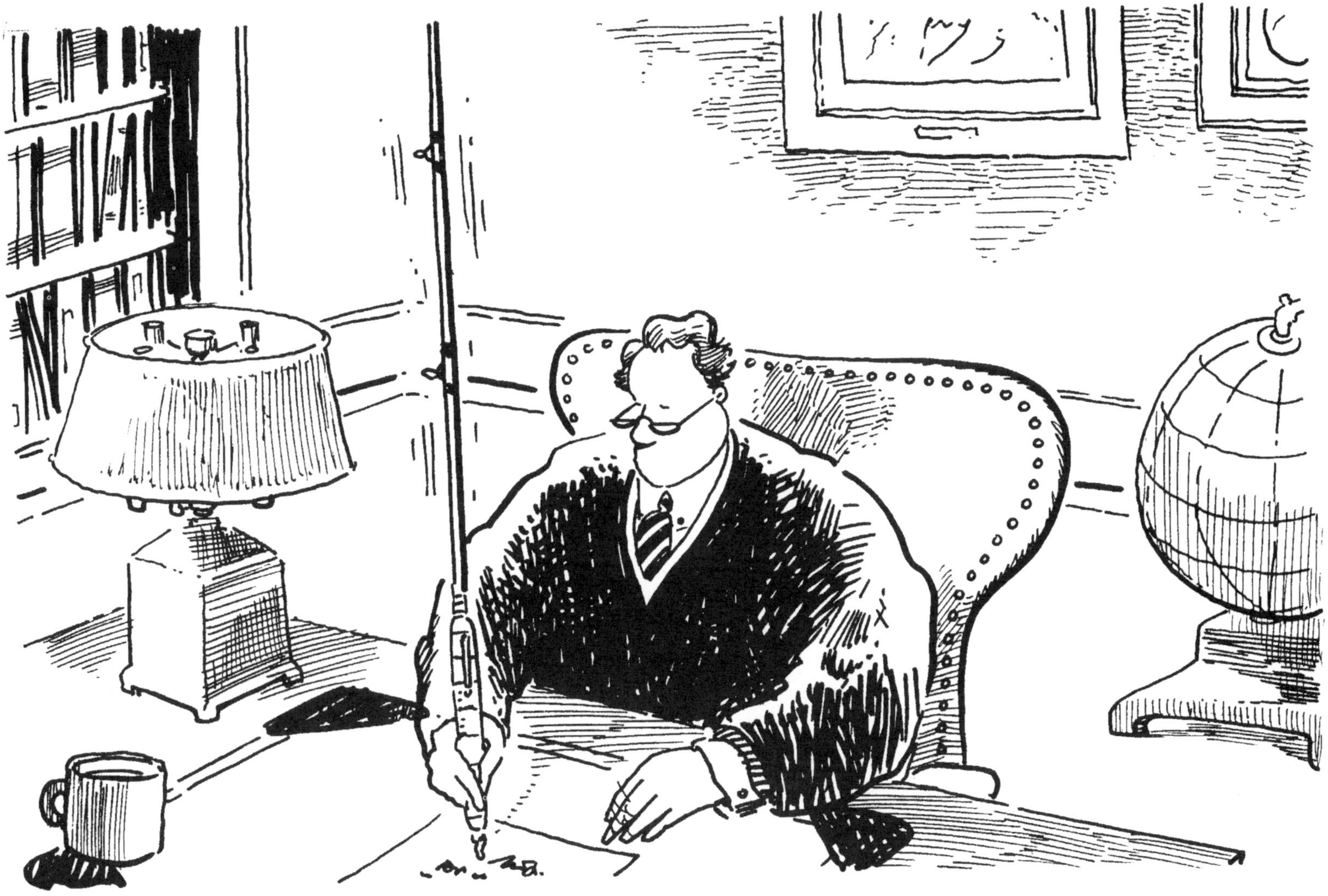

THE THING HAND VISE®

Tying flies at streamside can be an incredible pain. Normal hand vises are almost impossible to use, and may cause arthritis later in life. But not the Thing Hand Vise®: modelled after Thing from the hit 1960s sitcom and cartoon by New Yorker cartoonist Charles Addams, the Thing Hand Vise® is an actual hand! The Thing Hand Vise® doesn't just hold your flies, either. Just attach the convenient, easy-to-use harness, throw it around your neck, and the Thing Hand Vise® becomes your third hand in the river. It can hold your leader while you tie on a tippet, reach for a fly box or nippers during a heavy hatch while you're stripping and mending, and slap you silly when you've lost the big one.

Color: White, black, Asian.
Price: $49.95.

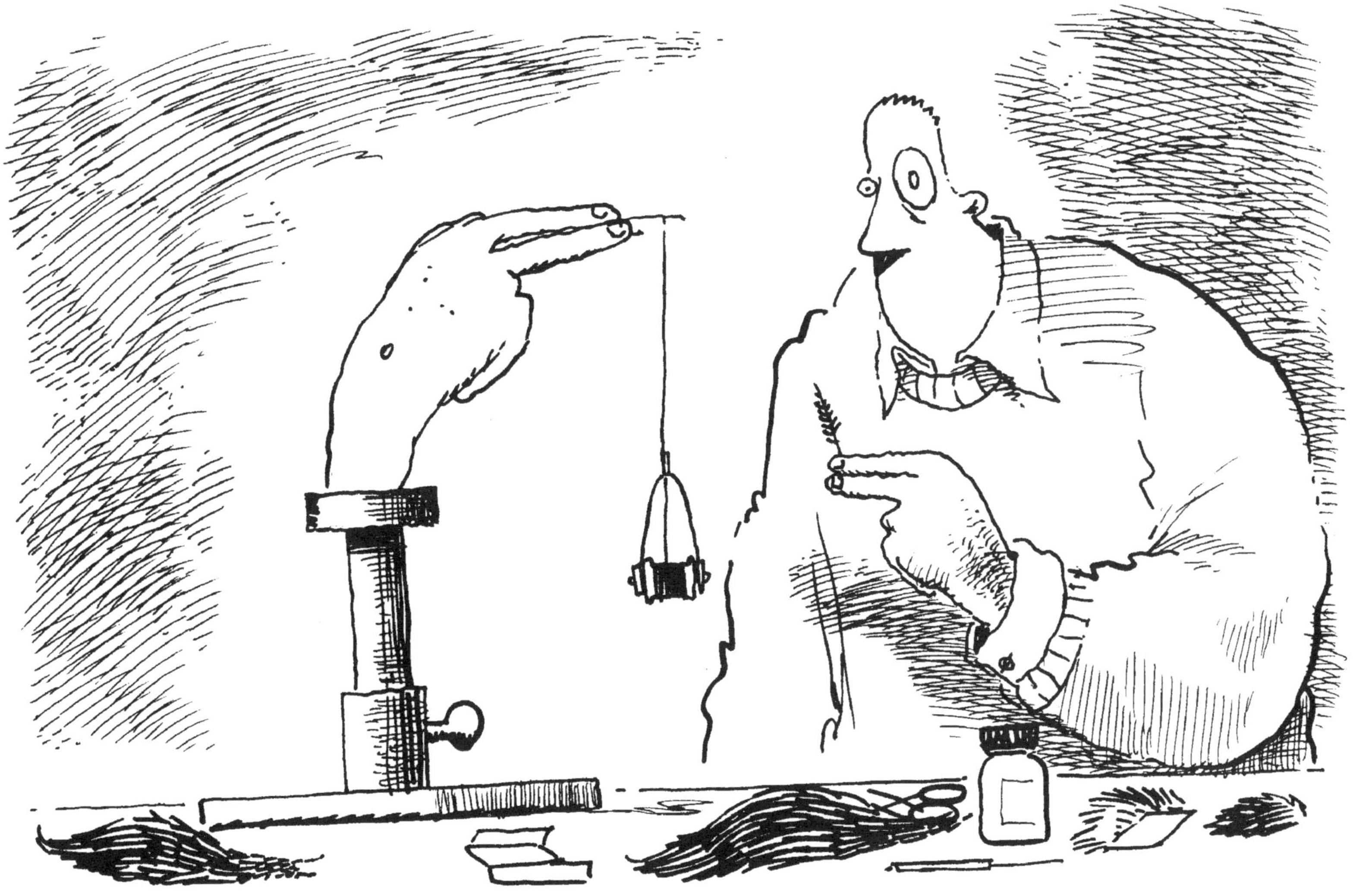

PRE-WRITTEN TROUT DIARY®

What's more frustrating than blank page after page of troutless days recorded in a genuine leather-bound, hand-tooled trout fishing diary? Do you want your grandchildren to discover years from now that you got blanked again on the Little Bearskin River? Save your progeny the embarrassment with the Prewritten Trout Diary®. America's finest fly fishing writers, ranging from John Geirach and Thomas McGuane, will personally write your entries, day after day, year after year, to create a fictional history of the ones that didn't get away. Imagine the lyrical prose, such as:

May 4, 1998   *The brilliantine light danced off the water of the Hammerhead River. Larks sang on the dusky banks as I hooked 34 gleaming, flashing rainbows ranging from four to eight pounds in a bit over one hour.*

Handwriting forgery experts will take our expert's writing and translate it into your own distinct hand, further adding to the harmless subterfuge.

Price: $1 per word, 9000 words minimum.

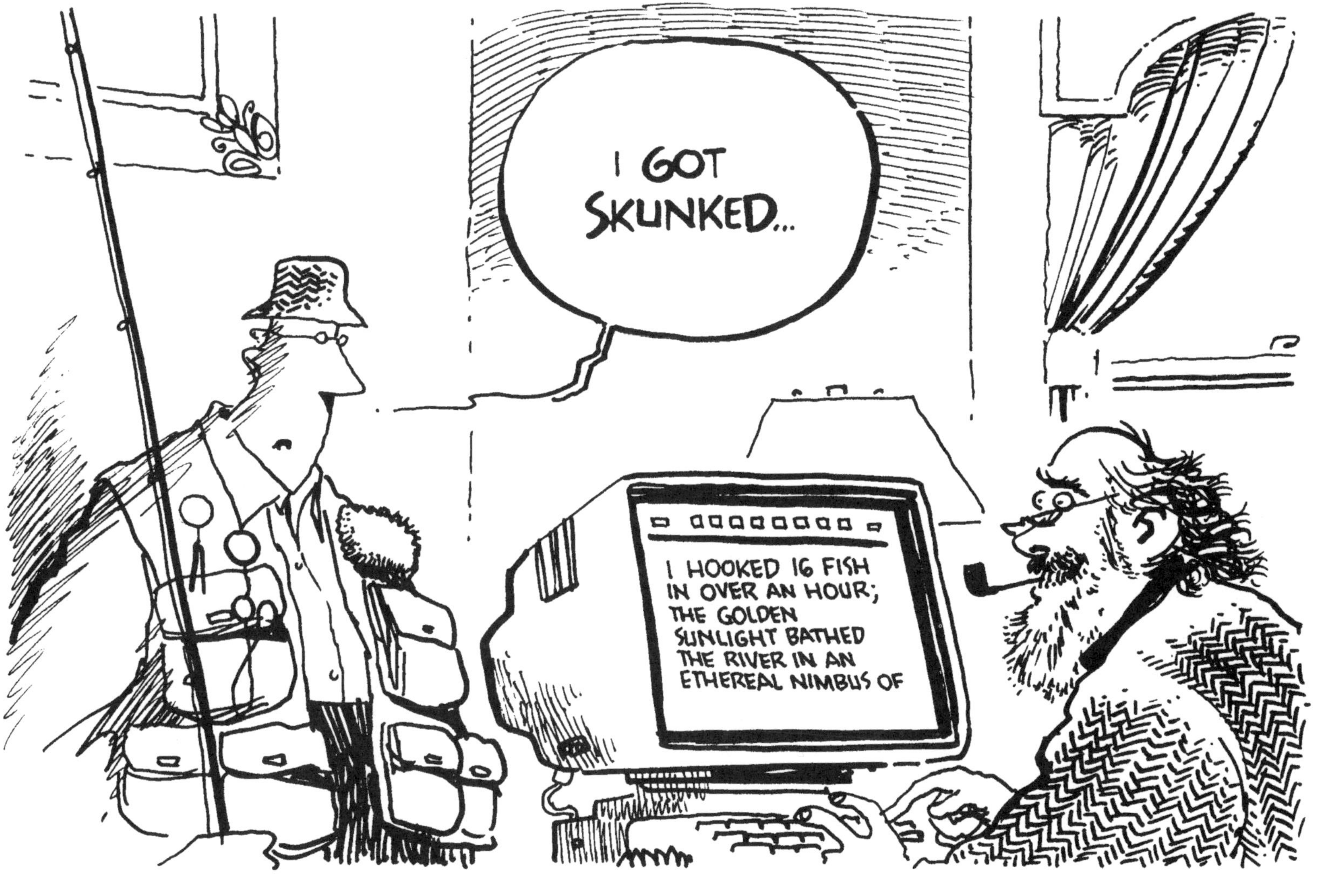
I GOT SKUNKED...
I HOOKED 16 FISH IN OVER AN HOUR; THE GOLDEN SUNLIGHT BATHED THE RIVER IN AN ETHEREAL NIMBUS OF

THE TROUT RIFLE®

Did you ever feel the need for a high-velocity firearm at streamside, either to ward off potential bait fishermen with friendly little warning shots or to pick off inconveniently located overhanging branches? Or maybe there's a particularly recalcitrant trout that won't come around to your way of thinking or your perfectly presented Quill Gordon. With the Trout Rifle®, tricky trout fishing situations become simple matters of gunplay. Rising trout jumping mockingly as you try fly after fly become suddenly more cooperative with a couple of 30.06 slugs fired into their feeding lanes. The adjustable baseball cap worm fishing crowd, with their jars of Dr. Gillslasher's Fish Ketchin' Aroma, littering cans of generic brand beer and nasty little Stryofoam bait containers, transform into tweedy Theodore Gordon-quoting cleanliness freaks with just one or two well-placed rounds. The Trout Rifle® is subject to state security background checks and all applicable federal weapon statutes in addition to any local laws regulating discharge of firearms.

Color: Walnut, or Tonkin cane stock.
Price: $465.
Price includes clip and a copy of *Mr. Bang-Bang's Safety Book and Streamside Hatch Guide*.

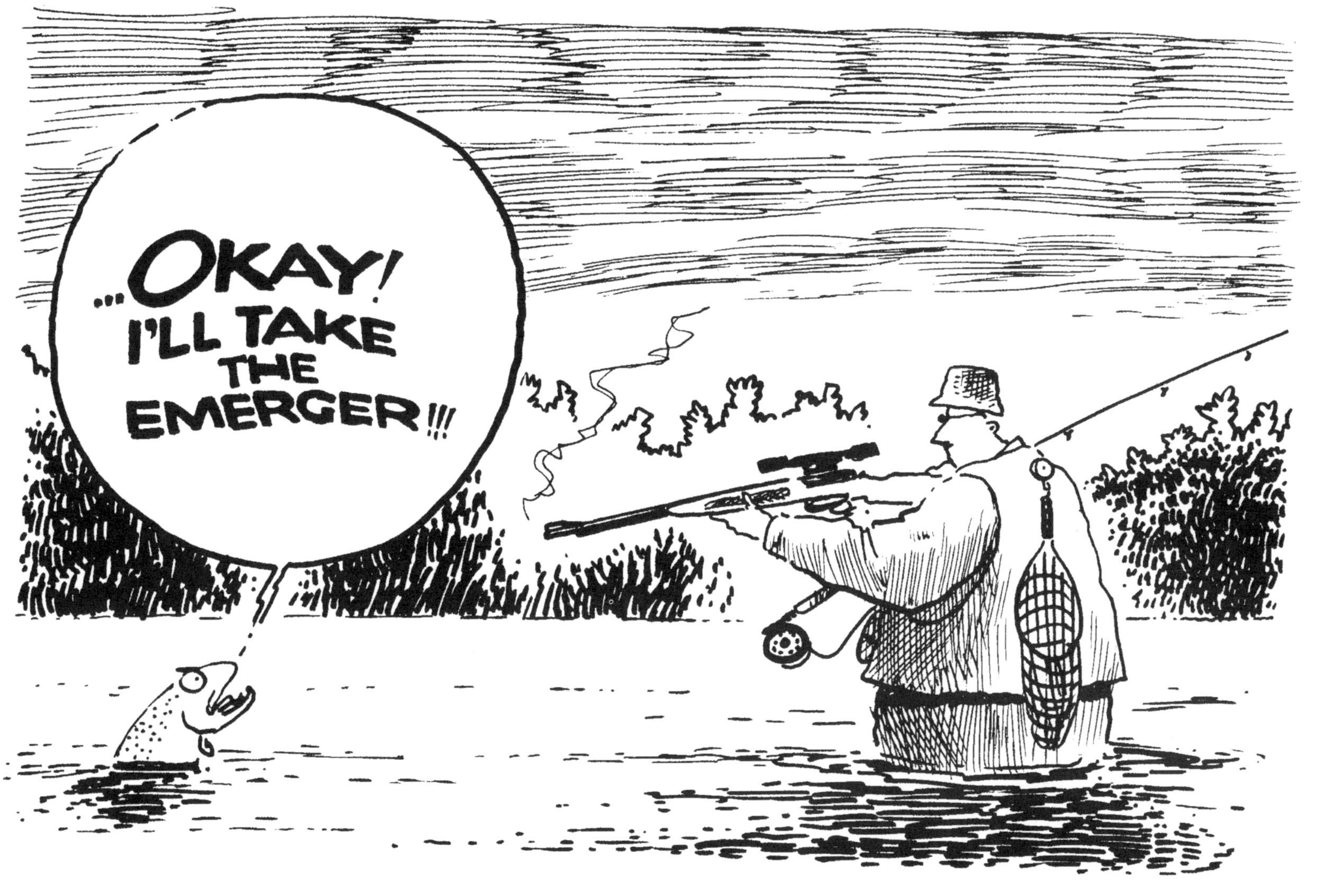
...OKAY! I'LL TAKE THE EMERGER!!!

STREAMSIDE ANALYSIS KIT®

Why do you fly fish constantly? Are you out of your mind? Obsessive about casting? Compulsive about leaders? Find out with the Streamside Analysis Kit®. A little known fact: Freud flyfished — dry! You've got to be certifiable to do that. Dr. Freud left behind a journal detailing his fishing disorder, and we've applied those principles in the Streamside Analysis Kit®. Kit includes couch, legal pad, cheap retractable pen, and a booklet with questions like, "Do you talk about long rods with your girlfriends?"

Color: Mood Indigo.
Price: $75 per hour.

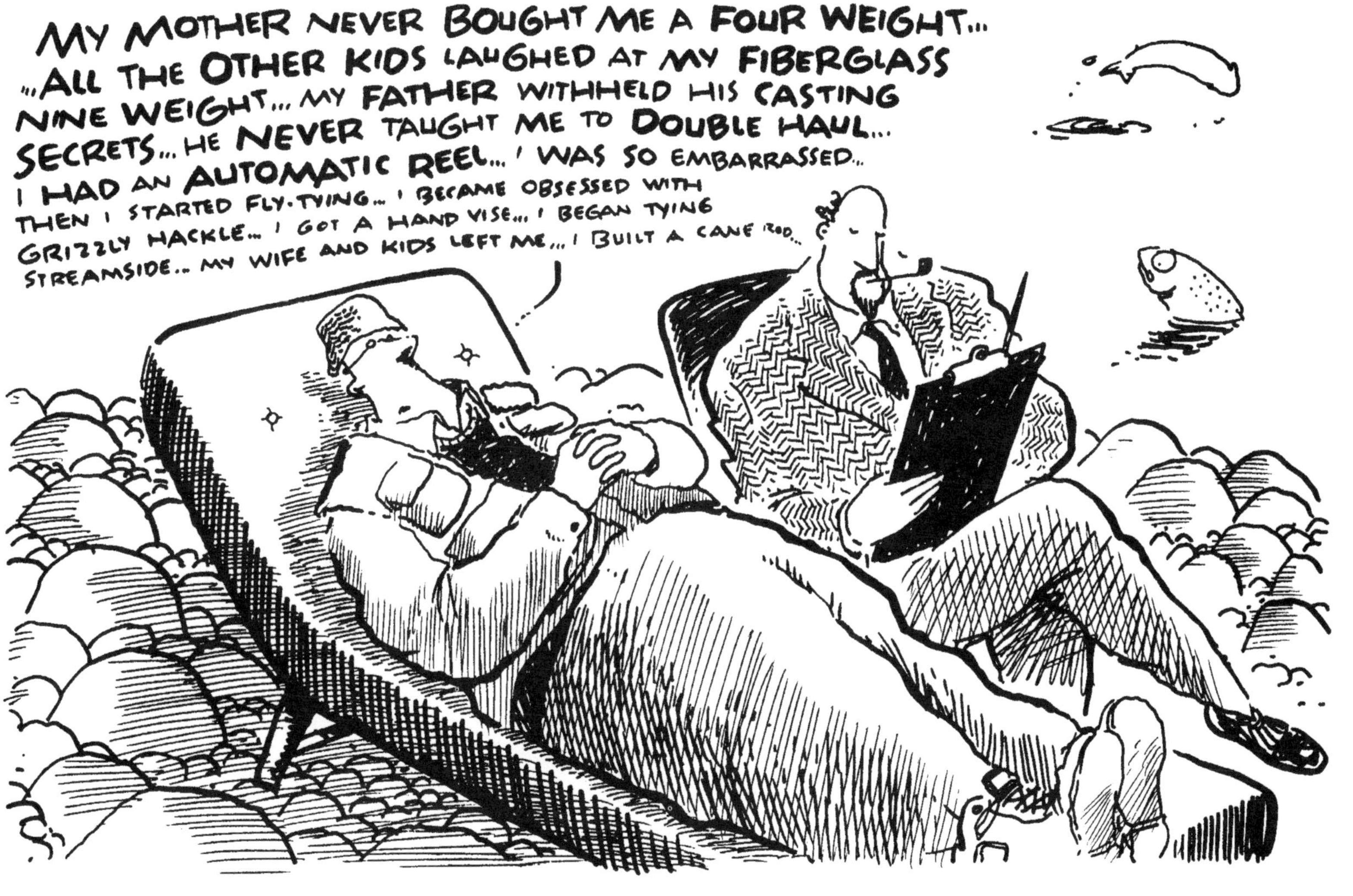

MY MOTHER NEVER BOUGHT ME A FOUR WEIGHT...
...ALL THE OTHER KIDS LAUGHED AT MY FIBERGLASS
NINE WEIGHT... MY FATHER WITHHELD HIS CASTING
SECRETS... HE NEVER TAUGHT ME TO DOUBLE HAUL...
I HAD AN AUTOMATIC REEL... I WAS SO EMBARRASSED...
THEN I STARTED FLY-TYING... I BECAME OBSESSED WITH
GRIZZLY HACKLE... I GOT A HAND VISE... I BEGAN TYING
STREAMSIDE... MY WIFE AND KIDS LEFT ME... I BUILT A CANE ROD...

CARP-TROUT CONVERSION KIT®

After a tough day at the stream, when trout only seem like an eastern establishment plot to separate you from your hard-earned bucks, you'll want to have a Carp-trout Conversion Kit®. Now you can fish any putrid Superfund site and turn those carp into gleaming, iridescent rainbow trout or buttery golden brown trout. The concept is simple: When you can't catch trout, tie on that doughball pattern, hook some fat carp, and you're ready to convert. You'll have a creel full of faux trout, ready to show off to even the most discerning fishing buddy. Perfect for photographs! Turn a radioactive thirty pound carp into a magnificent sea-run steelhead, fresh from the Pacific! Or make that stinking forty pounder into your state record brown!

The Trout-carp Conversion Kit® includes three cans of Krylon, a full pallet of Winsor Newton oil paints, and two pounds of bondo and a ball-peen hammer.

Price: $76.95

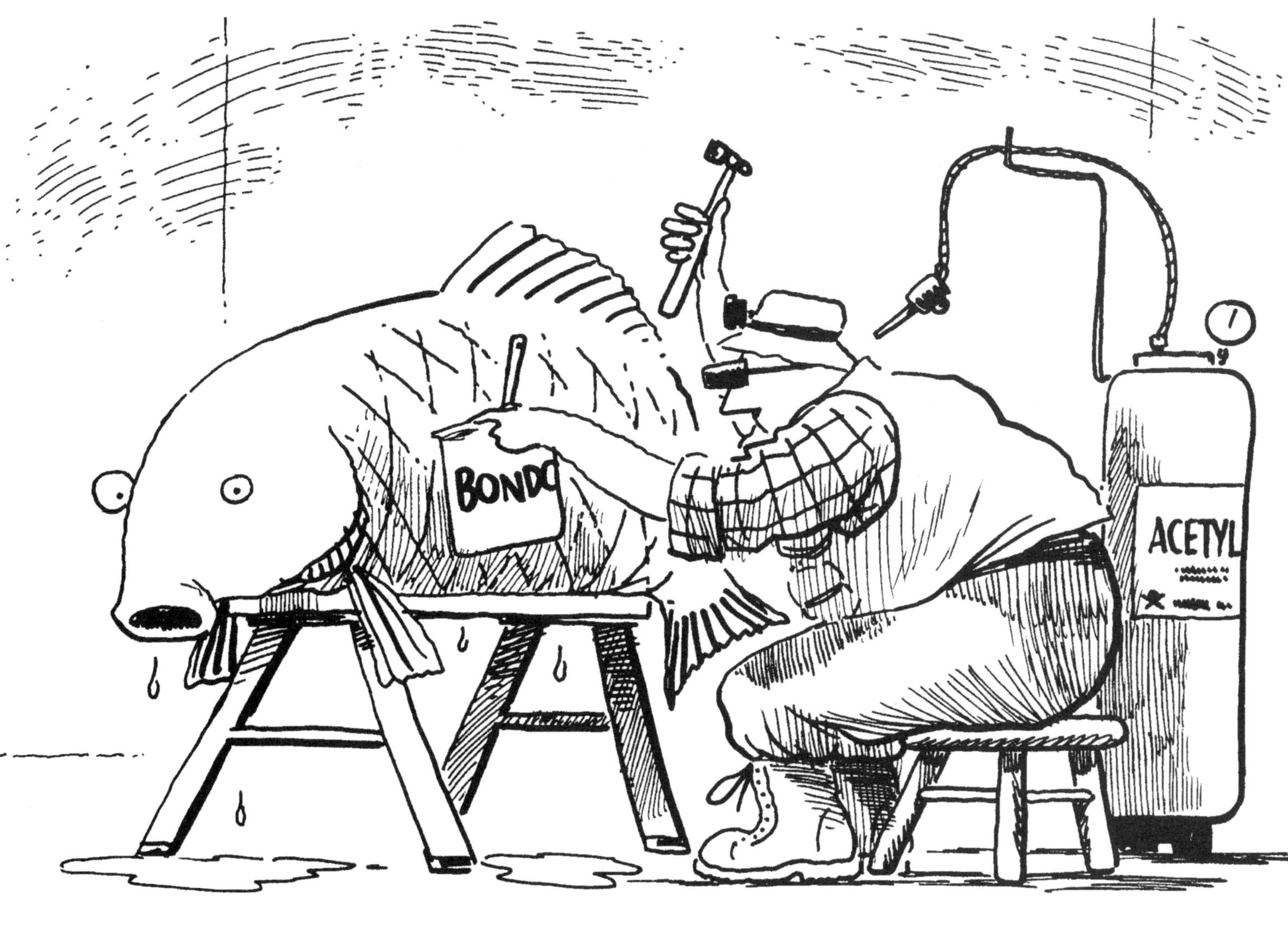
BONDO
ACETYL

THE BELLEVUE ISOLATION UNIT OBSESSIVE LEADER TYING KIT®

For years, mental health professionals have pre-scribed basket weaving as a therapy for their patients. Now there's a new therapy: leader tying! It's frustrating, irritating, and calls on the darkest impulses of the human spirit. Leader tying, simply put, will drive you crazy — but you'll never be able to stop. Why doesn't that blood knot stay together? If I make that fourth section too long, will my leader collapse on the water like a trick knee? Who says my butt section has to be thirteen inches long? In short, it's the perfect pur-suit to put you in the room with no sharp objects — and keep you there!

Price: $175 dollars per day, single patient occupancy. Does not include therapeutic drugs.

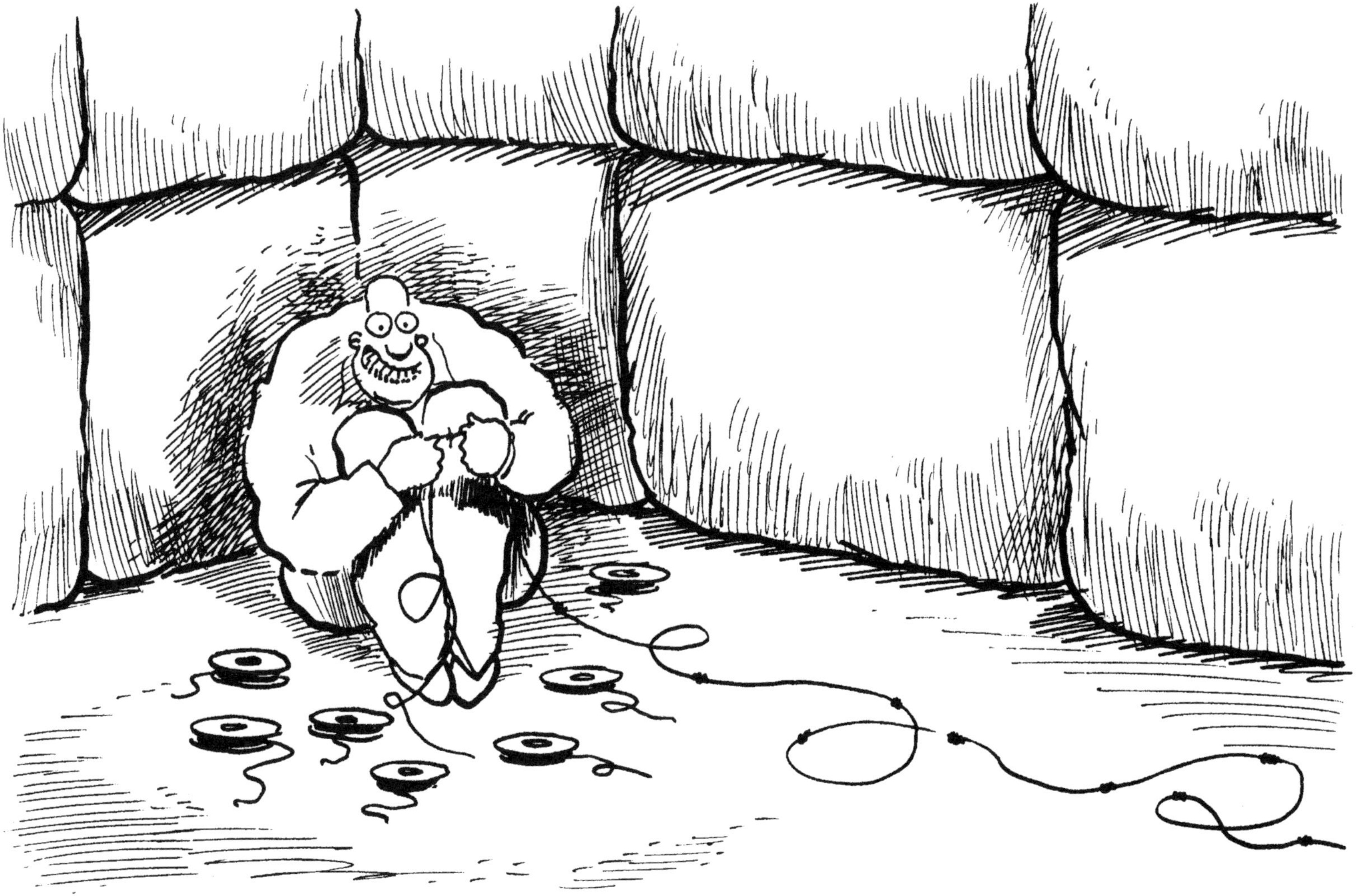

THE PEOPLE'S REEL®

Fresh from the former Soviet Union, and hand-crafted with the exacting care that Aeroflot engineers use. These reels were produced en masse for forty years at the Sverdlovsk People's Reel® Collective Factory and Potato Farm until the Berlin Wall came down. Constructed with attractive low-glare "Russian Army Olive" paint, with a gaily decorative Red Star in the center. Features include all-lead gears and lightweight balsa screws. Has the popular "No-Removal" spool system, which means you'll never lose another spool! Avoid any actual reeling. Makes an excellent paperweight.

Available in pallets of 900 only. Allow seven years for delivery.

Price: 6.7 billion rubles, or $2.99.

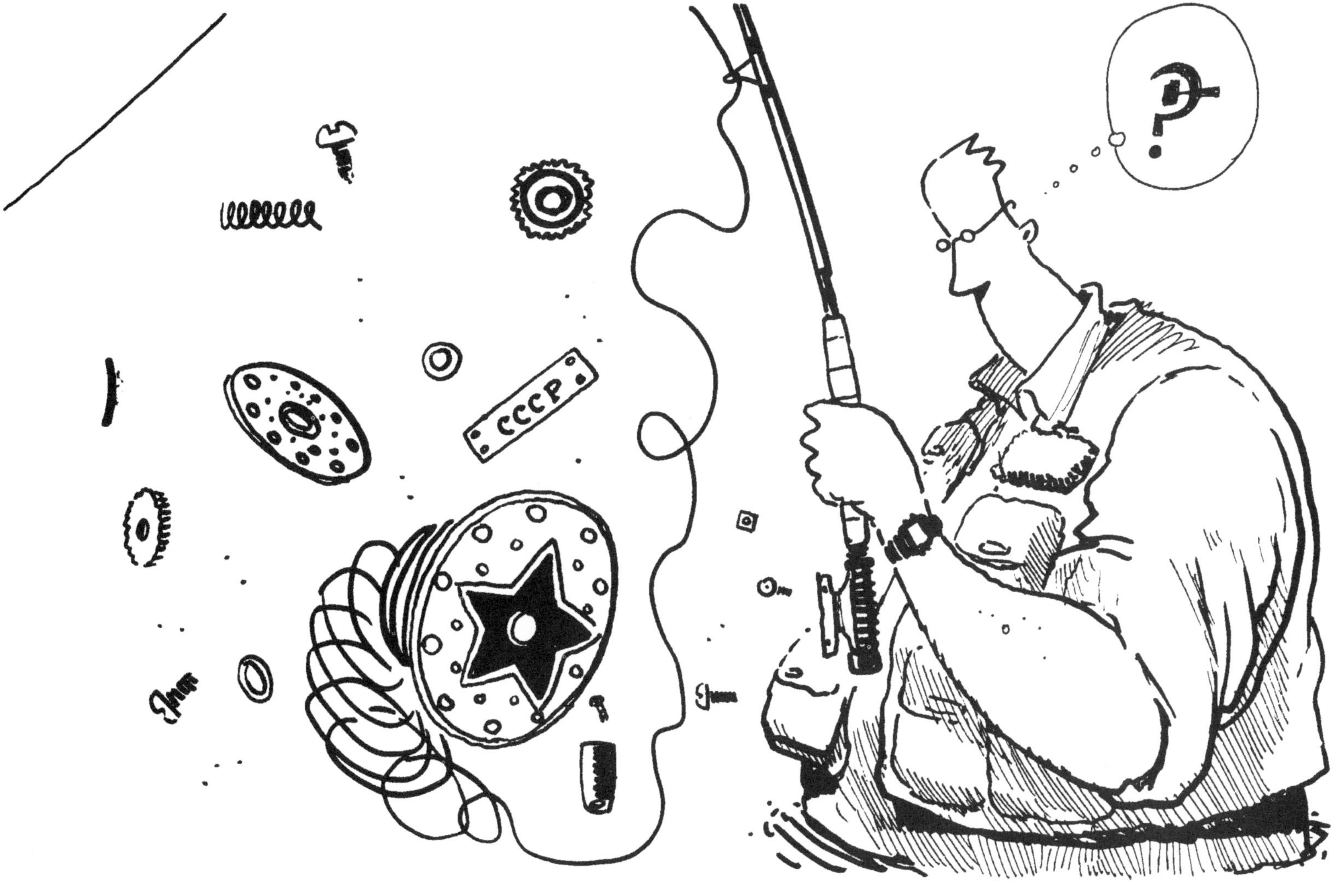
CCCP

THE CATCH 'N RELEASE NET®

The principle behind the catch and release net is simple: no net, no catch. Stop berating yourself over missed fish and empty creels: just stop catching fish. The Catch and Release Net® is easy to use; just place it under the trout and the line harmlessly snaps off; gently releasing the fish back into its native waters. He lives, and you have a clear conscience. You can't even get that from a shrink.

Price: $90.

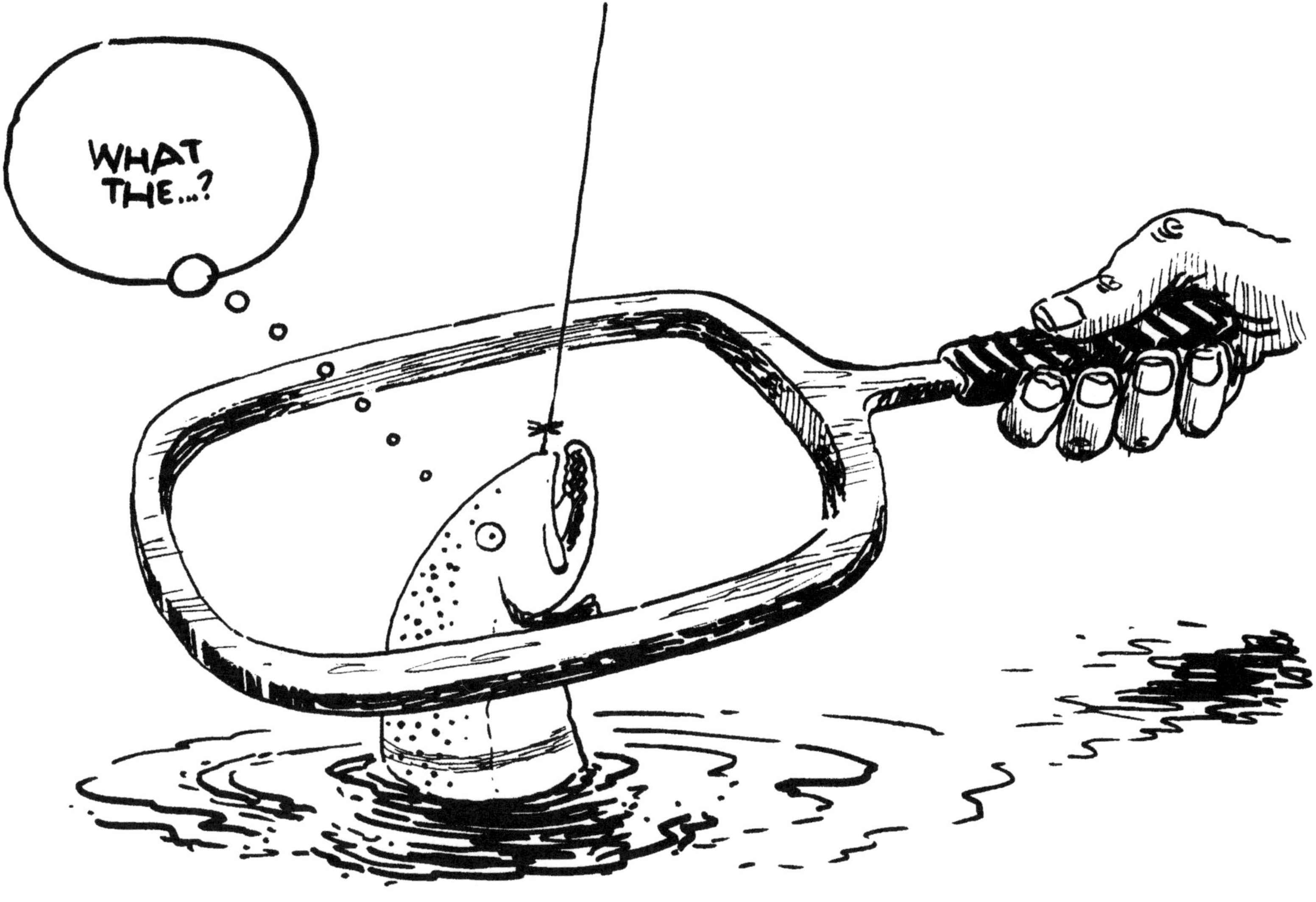
WHAT THE...?

FLY FISH RUSSIA

Imagine a ten-day guided fly fishing excursion into the Russian wilderness! Join experienced Russian guides who speak absolutely no English whatsoever, just like real American fly fishing guides. This trip takes you into the former worker's paradise to fish for the wily taimen, whatever that is. You'll hit all the great Russian rivers courtesy of Aeroflot, whose slogan is, "Nobody Lives Forever." You'll stay in deluxe accomodations that most Russian workers would never dream of, like snap-together shelter halves with no floors. You'll eat delicious authentic Russian cuisine, like newspaper soup and bread made during the Russian Revolution. Maybe you'll even snag Gregory Rasputin if you're using nymphs.

Ten-day trip: $2000.

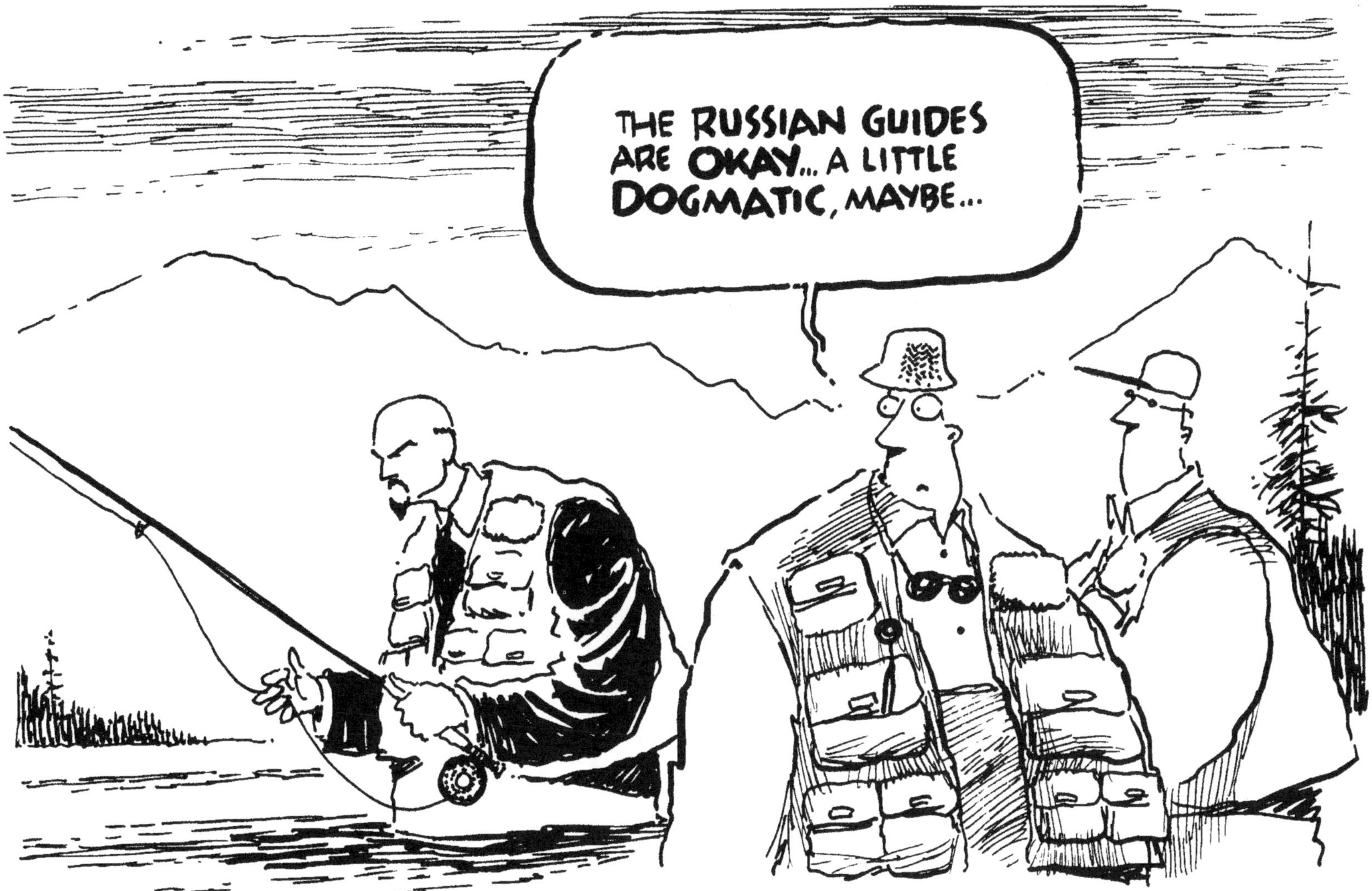
THE RUSSIAN GUIDES ARE OKAY... A LITTLE DOGMATIC, MAYBE...

BAIT FISHING INCOGNITO®

What real fisherman hasn't wanted to try a worm or salmon egg when all fly fishing hope is lost? Who hasn't secretly wished he could get rid of all his expensive gear and rig up with a nice fat red and white bobber and a Zebco? When you don't want to get caught bait fishing, just slip on the Bait Fishing Disguise, and your mother won't know you! Avoid the disapproving stares of your snob buddies. Includes adjustable plastic baseball cap with auto repair theme, t-shirt with a sexually suggestive slogan, jeans that reveal the upper reaches of your rear end, and a couple of warm cans of Rolling Rock, and a half-pack of Swisher Sweets.

Price: $12.99.

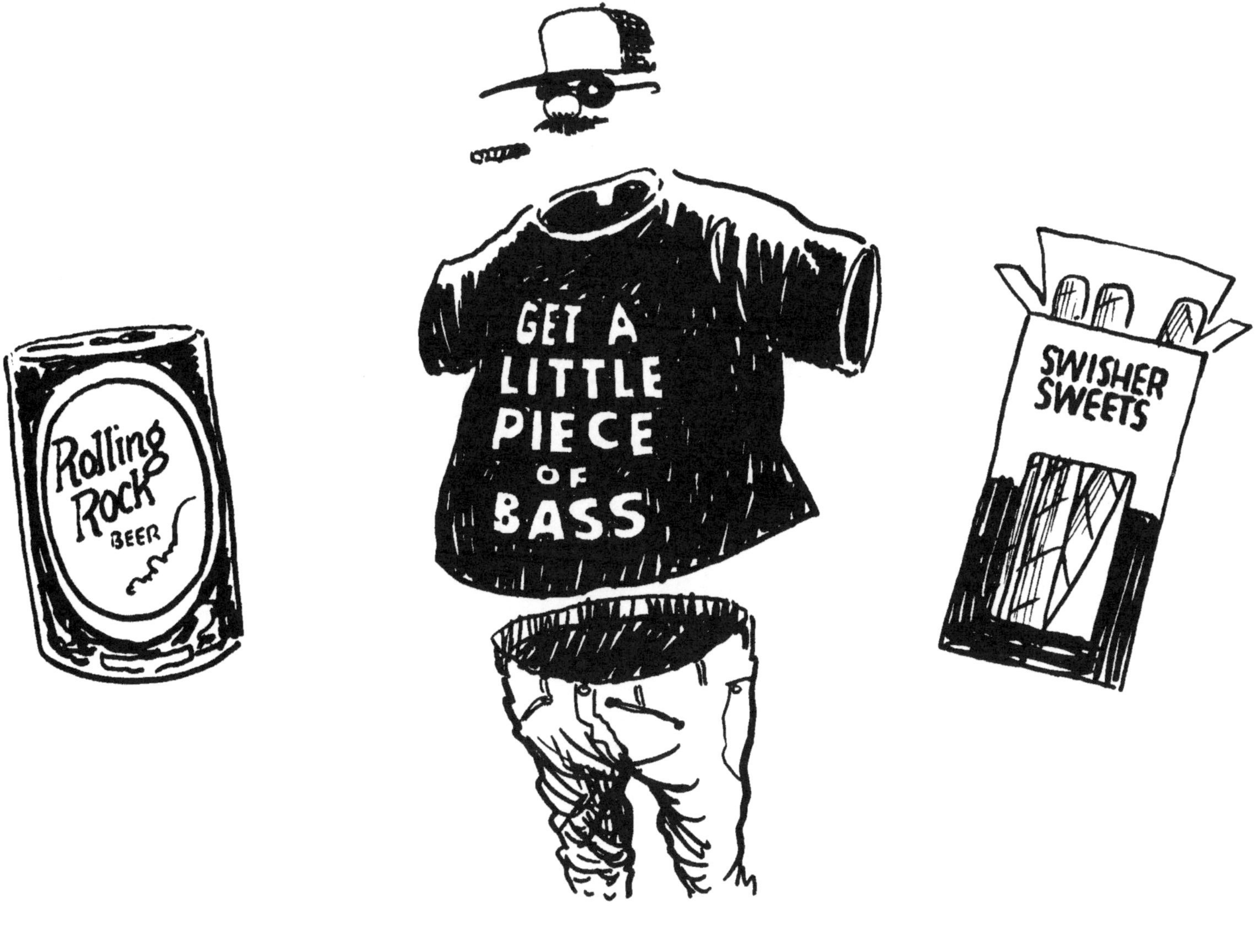

Rolling Rock
BEER
GET A LITTLE PIECE OF BASS
SWISHER SWEETS

TROUT RADAR®

You've had a fishless-so-far day. You haven't seen a riseform since the Carter Administration, and the light is getting long. You can't find the trout! Suffer no more with Trout Radar®, from General Salmo Dynamics, a division of Raytheon. With Trout Radar®, you can illuminate up to two miles of seemingly empty stream. Paint the trout you want, lock onto target, and you've saved the day, thanks to geosynchronous satellites and the handy heads-up display panel that clips to any standard size Orvis zinger. Why spend another frustrating day trying to locate working fish when you can use the same technology that won the Gulf War?

Price: $3.8 million.
Subject to black budget approval from the Pentagon and congressional appropriation. Presidential deniability is assured. CIA, Defense Intelligence Agency endorsed!

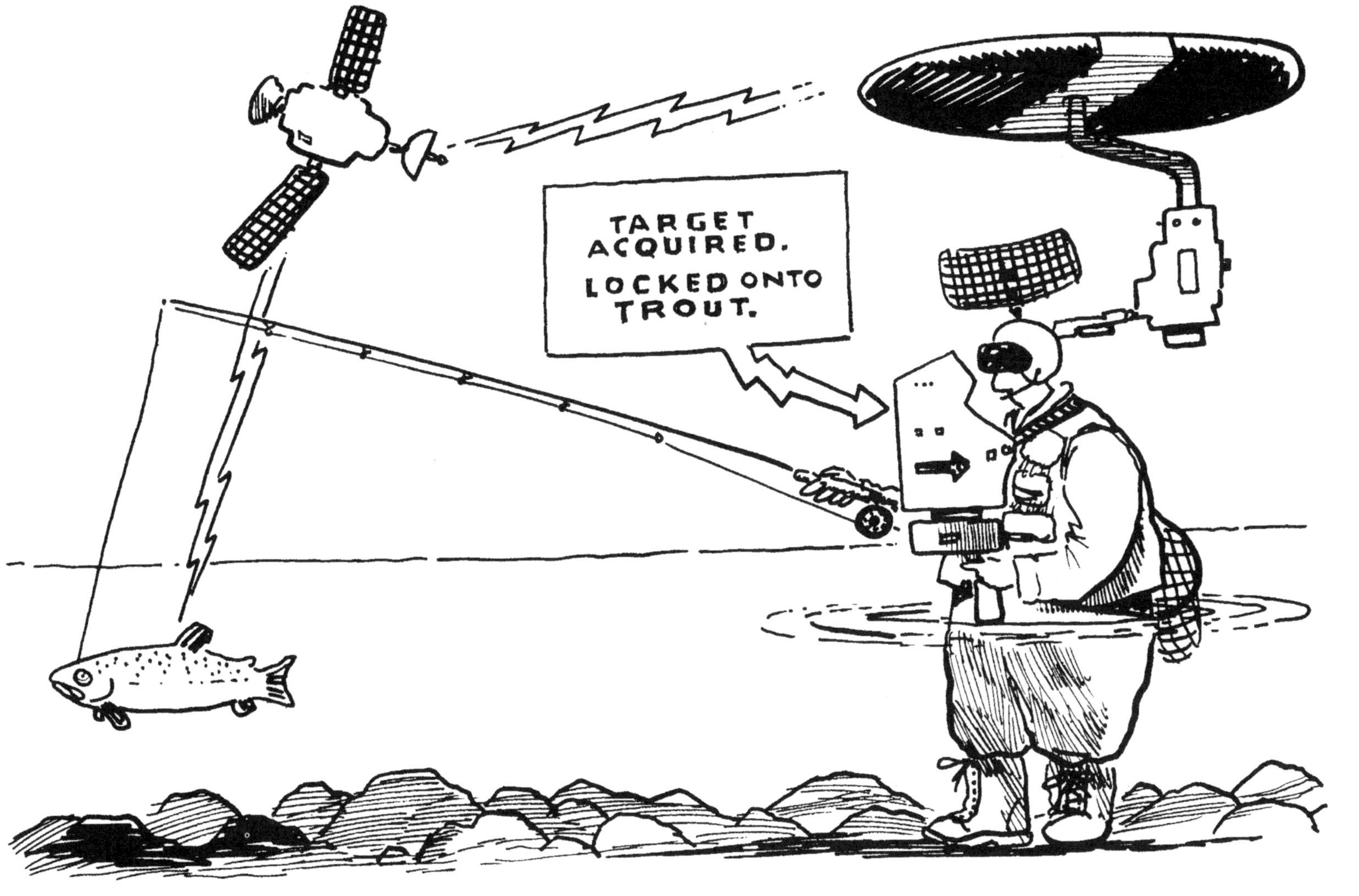
TARGET ACQUIRED. LOCKED ONTO TROUT.

THE LI'L HOOVER STREAM DIVERSION KIT®

Trout streams, with their irritating riffles, annoying back eddies that seem to switch time zones, and oddball cross currents that make drag free drift a concept only known to theoretical physicists, are the only obstacle between you and the fish. Eliminate the middleman with The Li'l Hoover Stream Diversion Kit®. The Li'l Hoover® sets up in no time and turns your favorite stream or river into a mucky mess full of flopping trout. Remember, trout are easier to spot when they're out of the water, and they'll take virtually any fly pattern out of sheer desperation. With the Li'l Hoover®, annoying math problems like calculating the CFS rate are eliminated, and you'll have minutes of fun before you kill all the trout.

Color: Concrete.
Weight: 3,785 tons.
Requires two AA batteries.
Price: $6,500,000.

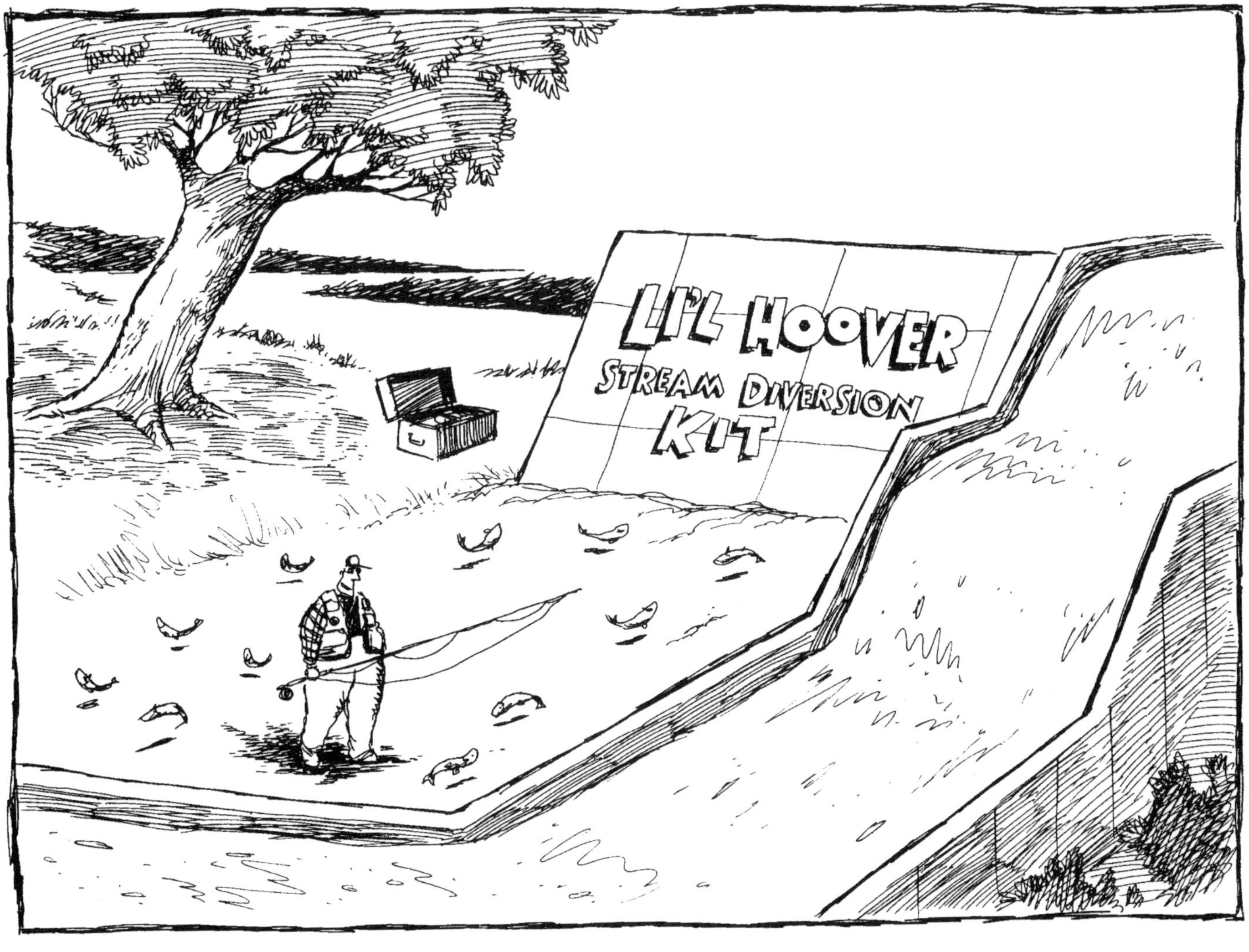
LI'L HOOVER
STREAM DIVERSION
KIT